What People Are Saying
Simply The Story

"The *Simply the Story* approach is effective because it helps us experience the story. The passage comes alive and each treasure you discover is fresh and powerful. It has been my joy to use it in many places and the response has always been very positive."

Babu Ganta - Communication Officer, Bible Society in the Gulf

---

"The world has been my address for 30 years, always with the goal of ministry 'multiplication.' Multiplication satisfaction came unexpectedly from a 79-year-old Chinese immigrant to Canada. He said:

> I wish I had had STS 40 years ago. We have not been raised as Christians to put well-thought-out questions to the Bible followed by discussion. Now, the Bible is like a new book for me.

"Ministry that lacks the empowerment to 'handle accurately the Word of God' for each and every Christian, is merely duplication. STS is a significant leader to fulfill the Great Commission."

Jim Thurber - Seminary Lecturer / Missions Trainer, Global

"*Simply the Story* training came into my life a few years ago, and was literally the answer to my prayers. I have served Jesus as a missionary for 35 years on several continents, with three of the world's main non-Christian religious groups, but I have ALWAYS struggled to share my faith in a natural way that fits the way God made me to be.

"This training literally changed my life and made evangelism and discipleship not only natural for me, but FUN! It is now 'freeing' and delightful to work with God's Holy Spirit and regularly see His Word cut deep to the core of people's lives. I am now really enjoying ministry, and seeing FRUIT from that ministry, like never before!"

Bryan Thompson - church planter/missionary/storyteller/podcaster with story4all, UK

"This 'oral inductive Bible study' should be a required subject in every Bible school and Christian institution! *Simply The Story* is a 'power tool' that will make any Christian more effective in communicating the Gospel."

Regina Manley - Oral Communications Specialist, Mission Aviation Fellowship, Global

---

"*Simply The Story* has been the best way for us to reach the unreached since we received our first training. This manual has given us the powerful means of making multiplying disciples and reignited in us a fresh desire to treasure God's Word. We learn Bible stories and store them in our heart pockets. Read this manual to discover STS and be equipped to become a practitioner. Your spiritual journey with the Lord will never be the same."

Rev. Apollos Djibo - Director Fufulde Ministries Training Centre, Niger

---

"One important strength of *Simply the Story* is that it depends on telling the stories in the teller's own words, but with great care to not add or subtract from Scripture. Another key point is that the story is then facilitated with questions to allow the Holy Spirit to reveal to the students the treasures in the story and their spiritual applications. This approach is very encouraging to the students and lets them realize that they too can share the Word of God with others accurately and in a way that brings Glory to God.

"Now their revolutionary idea of Oral Bible Schools is expanding the number of desperately needed church leaders all over the world."

Mike Holman - MAF Learning Technologies, Global

"I am serving as public journalist. I Thank God for the privilege to be part of TGSP and STS team to train hundreds of leaders in Karnataka. Learning God's Word through STS method helped me and my family to understand God's Word as it is and keep His Word in our heart and to share His Word (Story) where ever I go as public man."

M. Krishna, M.A. - Senior Journalist, Pal Voice Publisher, V J Pur, Karnataka, India.

"I have been working among Thai people for over 30 years. When I discovered STS I realized that this was an approach that truly resonated with the oral nature of this predominately Buddhist nation.

"The great need in this country is a church planting movement, which means that there must be an immediately transferable way to communicate biblical truth in an accurate yet culturally appropriate fashion. After teaching STS in various countries of Asia and in every part of Thailand, I have seen how suitable it is with preferred oral learners in rural communities but also in the more literate urban centers."

Larry Dinkins, ThM., PhD. - Bible Teacher, OMF Thailand

"WE have 60 orphans. Every day we find difficult to control these children because each one comes from different culture and different places. STS method helps us to teach them the Word God and now our Children are very good in Studies and growing spiritually and sharing His stories to their friends in their schools."

Rev. Vijay Raj - Executive Director Happy Home, Karnataka, India

---

"As an African missionary, church planter and Bible school teacher in my country, I recommend this manual to all laborers in Christian ministry. It is a detailed tool for anyone seeking to learn and teach the Bible orally to any person, anywhere in the World. *Simply The Story* for me starts at home. Every night before we go to bed, we learn and discuss a Bible Story together by applying the techniques in this manual. Our family is forever changed."

Rev. Jacob Ochieng Okoth - Showers of Blessings Church/Ministries, Founder, Kenya

---

"Dorothy Miller and the *Simply the Story* Team are trail blazers in the Bible Storytelling movement. I trained to become an STS Practitioner and have personally seen Bible stories come alive when presenting STS to both literate and oral learners."

Charles Cibene - CEO, MegaVoice, Global

"In STS I found the missing piece to ministry in Ethiopia and beyond. Their commitment to the veracity of Scripture prompted us to introduce this interactive way to share the Bible in Ethiopia. The story tellers are bringing people to Christ and more importantly, STS methods are transforming the lives of the storytellers as they delve into God's Word for themselves as the Holy Spirit guides them into all truth."

Julie Kay Field - Paraclete Mission Group Associate, Global

"I work among the Himalayan Tribal and our tribal people traditional practices depend on oral traditions since there were no written documents. Therefore the best way to communicate the Gospel to these tribal people is through storytelling. The storytelling (STS) is one of our best models to present the Gospel in our mountain state."

Rev. Tinuyangba Imchen - Senior Pastor / Bible Teacher, Arunachal Pradesh, India

---

"STS helped us to understand God's Word as it is easy to understand and remember full story and keep it in our heart pocket. It helped us train our local Church non-literate elders to learn God's Word and to reach their neighboring families and villages. STS method helped us plant more Churches then before."

Rev. Devasahayam – Senior Pastor/Church Planter, F L Church, Andra Pradesh, India

---

"I was struck by the biblical accuracy that was maintained in simply telling, retelling and examining the stories for the observations and applications found in them. Anytime that someone—in this very interactive, dialogic process—brought forth something that was even the slightest bit 'off,' the moderator (storyteller) would simply say, 'Can we find that in the story?' Immediately the group was brought back to the Word and it was easily sorted out."

Pastor Miles DeBenedictis - Cross Connection, USA

"As a Bible scholar and theologian, I see STS as the most effective means to do biblical exegesis. In my 24 years of discipleship ministry in my country, I just now realized that I have never discipled one person who could not read and write. The skills in this STS manual have helped me to get started with that monumental task. I recommend every page to all people, especially my fellow theologians."

Rev. Luvao - Jerusalem New Life Pentecostal Church International, D.R. Congo

---

"I have seen the growth of The God's Story Project India from its inception. We have seen people's lives changed through the power of simplicity and reproducibility of the Bible stories. I am convinced that if we want to reach this nation for the Lord in our generation, we need to teach, train and disciple the people the way they understand. I strongly recommend every Church planter to get hold of this training and use Bible Stories to disciple our nation for Christ."

Rev. Dr. Sam Abraham - Director Himachal Bible College, Berachah Ministries, India

Simply The Story
Inductive Bible Study "Oral Style"

STS Handbook

Exploring Scripture Through Discussion
Listening and Responding

Dorothy A. Miller
The God's Story Project

Contents

Forward: Africa

I met Dorothy Miller at a crucial consultation in the Gulf a few years ago. There she introduced the glory of telling God's story to my wife and ME as a good strategy to reach out to people, even in restricted areas. We went through a simple story of Mary and Martha together and it was so amazing how much treasure there WAS in it.

Subsequently, I bought into the idea, and we introduced it to a few Calvary Ministries (CAPRO) fields in Nigeria, with tremendous reports of impact. Calvary Ministries (CAPRO) is an indigenous mission agency focusing on Church Planting among unreached people groups in 30 countries in Africa. We have Church planting work among 65 UPGs and MUPGs.

One can discover that, from one generation to the next, God reveals Himself to people in various ways. We have these evidences encapsulated in the stories that are in the Bible. His appearance in Christ and Holy Spirit epitomizes His love for mankind, and will to help man find this treasure.

Simply The Story (STS) is a means of systematic exploration of the Bible. With it, both literates and illiterates are helped to dig into the Word of God inductively.

The African culture of storytelling is a potent avenue to inculcate values and pass down life changing instructions. As a result, it provides a familiar ground for listeners, especially in rural areas, where the majority live and enjoy the oral tradition.

Beyond this harmony, STS helps listeners arrive at independent conclusions, which give ownership to the decisions they arrive at following personal discovery. What helps this to happen most, is the approach of the story teller and the series of questions that are posed to the listeners. These enhance the communication of spiritual biblical truth across cultures in an accurate way.

The two approaches of exploring spiritual observations and spiritual applications prompt listeners to quest. This method enables listeners to understand and remember biblical truths embedded in the stories, which form a significant percentage of the Bible.

In addition, STS provides sufficient caution for story tellers on comportment while telling stories. It emphasized the need to explore the setting, content and implication of the stories they hear.

Apart from catchy statements from beneficiaries of the STS training across the world, the book provides a lot of tips in the form of questions that are helpful for personal exploration of the Bible stories.

I have no reservation in recommending the STS training for all who receive the call to make disciples of all nations, particularly among oral communities and those who desire personal revival in their relationship with God.

Amos Aderonmu - International Director, Calvary Ministries (CAPRO)

Forward: United States

We have known and been best friends with Dorothy and Tom Miller for more than 40 years. It has been remarkable to witness the birth and rapid growth of first the movie, *God's Story,* and then the training, *Simply The Story*.

We rejoice in seeing how this ministry is changing the face of the ways Christians can reveal Christ to the lost, disciple others, and be discipled by the Word of God.

We have been encouraged to see these techniques sweeping through villages and nations around the world, bringing new inspiration and excitement about the Word of God. The storytelling format appeals to everyone, everywhere.

The inductive Bible study methods of STS draw insight and instruction from the participants themselves resulting in a far richer and deeper experience of the Scriptures than is the norm. The cutting edge techniques of STS reach people.

In fact, the wide range of people being reached with the true message of the Gospel regardless of age, nationality, religious background, education, level of literacy or any other consideration shows *Simply The Story* as completely unique and exceptionally effective.

This ministry especially touches our hearts because it reaches those frequently left on the perimeters looking in—without means, without skills, without influence. With its powerful ability to reach in and touch the spirit of anyone, literate or nonliterate, rich or poor, privileged or underprivileged, it is the best and most effective tool for advancing the Kingdom that we have seen in all our years of ministry around the world.

Don and Sondra Tipton – Founders & Directors, Friend Ships Unlimited

The profound truths from God are housed in the simple stories of the Bible.

God's Word warns that our minds can be led away from the "simplicity that is in Christ" (KJV, 2 Corinthians 11:3).

Acknowledgements

In the Bible, our Lord God revealed Himself and His will to us. We thank God His Word. The Lord designed us to serve Him and to deliver His Word; for that privilege we give thanks, and give Him all the glory for any ministry effectiveness.

God has sent to The God's Story Project many thousands of volunteer servants who have produced hundreds of language versions of *God's Story*. We thank Him for the orchestrators, translators, narrators, recordists, funders and users of *God's Story* who come from a pool of missionaries, indigenous workers and just wonderful people who love Jesus!

For the office workers and organizers in various countries, who serve so vitally, and sometimes do so unnoticed except by God, we praise Him. We include those whose work, ideas and stories are in the handbook. For the growing core of *Simply The Story* directors and instructors, we stand in awe and thank God. We praise the Lord for the vast army, now in the millions, who bravely and boldly are telling His stories worldwide.

In 1994, artist Norm McGary painted ten biblical pictures. He used his skill to depict Jesus as the "I Am" in hopes that his elderly mother might trust Jesus as her God and Savior. Norm went home to Jesus in 2012 and joined his mother there. His art became *God's Story*, which prompted the development of *Simply The Story*. We love Norm for his servant's heart. We praise the Lord for the way one man's love of Jesus and desire to see his mother saved has exploded into a world outreach.

Tom and Dorothy Miller
The God's Story Project

Chapter 1: The Need for Oral Strategy

As a Bible teacher in secular and Christian environments in the western world, my desire was to present the Bible in a way that it could be understood and would change lives.

I came to see that chronological presentation and the discussion of story passages fulfilled that desire. Especially when people were guided by questions, but still allowed to discover for themselves, they understood and made personal applications from the Bible.

God opened the door for me to author the film, *God's Story: From Creation to Eternity*. That film used the chronological, story approach to present the Bible to a world audience. We saw the impact of this 80-minute, storytelling overview as it went out in hundreds of languages. That film, and even the usefulness of its audio track, made us keenly aware of the central place of story in evangelism and discipleship.

Later, we connected with other mission leaders who had started emphasizing the importance of staying in one story. They had recognized the need to broaden their methods of presenting Scripture to include those in the world who did not, or could not, learn from reading. The insights we gained from these other leaders prompted us to combine discussion-style teaching with staying in one story at a time. That combination became *Simply The Story* (STS).

STS stays in one story, and goes deeply into the Word. Through targeted discussion questions, people discover for themselves. We now see more than understanding and personal application. We see—remembering!

**He who drives the wagon to town
knows the way back the next time.**

And even beyond those results, we see that people are empowered and emboldened to share with others.

STS encourages presenters of Bible information to utilize stories the way God gave them, as whole stories. When we refer to "stories," we include multiple passages in the Bible, even passages that do not at first appear to be story. This handbook offers information on how to tell those stories interestingly and accurately and how to teach them using discussion. Besides this handbook and other media resources, the personalized coaching provided in STS workshops helps people develop these skills.

Who Needs This Style of Learning Scripture?

A man who came to an STS workshop in the USA explained why he was there:

> One year into my first pastorate, I realized there was a serious problem. I had a four-year degree in Bible from Charleston Southern University and had earned a master's degree from Gordon-Conwell Theological Seminary with highest honors. I was ready to teach and train. I wanted to fulfill the great commission in the place God gave me to serve. Things were going well from the pulpit. People nodded their heads and said at the door, "Good sermon, preacher."
>
> Within a few months, several new believers began gathering in a Sunday school class developed just for them. They had come to faith, but now they needed to learn more to grow. We gave them the standard written material from our denomination's publishing house, the "Quarterly." I encouraged them, "Go home and read over this material. When you come back, we can talk about it."
>
> Week after week in the class I would ask them, "What did you learn from what you read? Do you have any questions? Did you find anything interesting?" Almost always the answer was—silence.
>
> It became apparent that they were not reading the lessons. Finally one week, out of frustration, I asked someone to start our class by reading the lesson out loud. After a very long and awkward wait, one man volunteered. He struggled through a few lines very slowly and mispronounced many words. Then I knew! These people were not reading the lessons—because they could barely read.
>
> As I looked into this further, statistics confirmed what I had seen. Nearly one third of the adults living around my church did not have a high school education. As a young pastor I was faced with a difficult question: how can we evangelize and disciple people who cannot or prefer not to read?
>
> Unfortunately, I was unequipped to answer this question. Even after spending seven years preparing for ministry at two evangelical institutions, I never once heard anything about oral learners. I had no idea that low literacy would be a challenge in ministry and I had no tools to work with these

oral learners whom God called me to pastor. This is why I came to be trained.

That pastor and other people who come to STS workshops share three common values: they treasure God's Word, they desire to understand, remember and apply Scripture to their lives, and they want to nurture those things in the lives of others.

How Big Is the Need for Oral Communication?

The value of presenting Bible stories in their entirety takes on greater importance when we recognize what the classification of "oral learner" means and how oral learners gain information.

People who cannot read are, by default, oral learners. Upon investigation, one sees that most countries either inflate their literacy rates or publish rates based on poor measurements of literacy, such as "If you can sign your name, you are literate!"

Multiple tests and research, such as the National Assessment of Adult Literacy study, show that 43% of people in the USA are unable to read or cannot read well enough to understand the meaning of a full paragraph of text. Additionally, another 44% of people in the USA prefer to exchange information by listening and discussing. These surprising statistics hold true for other developed nations as well. This means that 87% of the people in developed nations either cannot learn using literate methods, or they are preferred oral learners.

In developing nations, where opportunity to go to school is limited, the literacy rate is much lower. So the percentage of nonliterate or preferred oral learners within those countries is even higher.

Oral learners do not, or cannot, take notes, so the way they remember information is by weaving it into a story. Information presented to oral learners in concepts, precepts, topics or outline form has no story, so the people's framework for remembering is missing.

Note God's emphasis on story in the way He designed the Bible. The Bible is:

10% exposition
15% poetry and
75% narrative (story)

Have you ever tried to share an incident with someone, but the person kept interrupting you all the way through, asking questions and making comments? By the time you completed your story, it had lost its impact due to the multiple interruptions. Bible stories also carry their maximum power when they are presented whole, as they are written. Since God gave 75% of the Bible to us in story format, perhaps we should let the Lord tell His whole story?

Pitfalls of Current Most-Used Methods

Imagine wrapping a gift and sending it to a friend, and then later it comes back to you unopened! Should you assume that your friend did not want the package's contents? Could it be that your intended recipient did not know how to open the package?

When we wrap biblical truths in a topical, conceptual or analytical package, those who primarily are oral learners simply cannot open it.

It is time for those of us who desire to communicate biblical truth to consider the consequences of losing "the story." The vast majority of people who need to hear the Gospel and need discipleship are oral learners. When we as communicators step outside of story and restructure and reorganize information, oral learners not only cannot remember that information, most of them will not even have understood the truths that we presented.

Why Use *Simply the Story*

One of the major differences between the conventional, topical way of teaching and this STS way of storytelling with inductive study, oral style, is reflected in this vital question. Who or what is going to teach? Let's look at the biblical roles of the teacher, the student, Scripture and the Holy Spirit.

In topical teaching, the presenter decides ahead of time what is going to be taught. Verses or passages are selected by the teacher and given to the listeners to illustrate and authenticate the teacher's views. This method is not wrong—but it is not the only way to teach.

Topical teaching breaks up a story, making the information more difficult to remember. Bible stories speak to our spirit, soul and body. The more a teacher breaks apart the story and presents information in categories, the more the information goes only to our minds, not our souls and spirits.

When teaching topically, the presenter selects passages from throughout the Bible to verify pre-selected points. The congregation listens and might take notes. But, with this approach there is no story to follow. So for those who cannot take notes, there is nothing to keep the information together. For them, it is like a human body with no bones!

Since the oral learners in the congregation have no way to remember what was taught, they are not able to pass on much of the information to others. Without a story to follow, nothing connects the information together.

And the literate learners—what about them? Without consulting their notes, most of them too will not be well equipped to share the message, and frankly, most church goers do not carry those sermon notes with them in the market places of life. However, both types of learners, literate and oral, can pass on any good testimonies and story examples that were used to illustrate the sermon!

Also, most of the listeners have no way to find that kind of topical information on their own, so dependency on the teacher is perpetuated. Morsels of information are handed to the listeners much the same as a mother bird gathers food and then drops it into the open mouths of her waiting babies. Each week these listeners wait for their next meal. Too much topical teaching creates fifty-year-old birds in a nest!

Another pitfall in the overuse of topical teaching is this. Teachers most often choose a subject to present that they think people need to hear. The tendency then is to select verses from throughout the Bible that the teachers already know. The topical method just does not press teachers to explore less familiar passages for information and insights.

Most believers have been to a Christian conference. Topics presented may be ones such as evangelism, reaching Unreached People Groups, family, finances, abstinence, prayer, attributes of God, healing, integrity in business or prophecy. All are important topics. Interestingly, we see that all of these topics can also be covered through the presentation and discussion of stories.

In the oral, inductive type of storytelling, the teacher uses the whole story and lets the content of the story determine the insights and lessons to be taught.

When teachers decide ahead of time which topic will be taught from a Scripture passage or story, the rest of the information in the selected Scripture can easily be overlooked. But when a story is fully explored and developed through questions and discussion, multiple topics will be discovered and discussed. The Holy Spirit delivers personalized messages to each person as He determines.

In general, topical teaching, with its list of Scripture passages and verses that verify teaching about that topic, unintentionally can deliver biblical information to the hearer as a rule or a law. When stories are used, the spirit of the entire story or passage is allowed to speak to the hearers.

information to the hearer as a rule or a law. When stories are used, the spirit of the entire story or passage is allowed to speak to the hearers.

At times, teachers think they are using the STS method, when in reality they are missing the vital ingredient that makes an STS-taught story touch many lives. They make this mistake. The teacher tells the story and then makes the story speak to a topic that the story may not even be addressing.

The story is made to fit the teacher—rather than the teacher fitting to the story. In genuine STS, whatever insights you teach must be seen in the story.

When teachers use a story just as a platform to teach what they already know and believe, they lose the blessed opportunity to be taught new information by the Holy Spirit. Discovering new treasures in a story is thrilling for teachers. The challenge for the storyteller-teacher becomes how to gently offer their newly-found treasures in the form of questions so that their listeners too can experience that thrill of discovery.

Vital Decision. If our goals are to clearly communicate biblical truths in developed nations, and to do all we can to reach both the lost in the 10/40 window and among the Unreached People Groups of the world, a radical change must take place in the way we present our information. Will we respond? (See the book *Making Disciples of Oral Learners.* It is available for download in print and audio format at www.oralbible.com.)

Chapter 2: Questions and Stories – Biblical Precedent

The Jesus Model: Tell The Story, Ask Questions

How did Jesus teach? Out of the almost 200 times Jesus was asked a question, He only responded with a direct answer a few times! Nearly all of the other times Jesus responded by asking a question, or telling a story or parable. Also, did Jesus just tell a story and move on? ... No. Usually, after telling the story, He asked a question and invited discussion.

Did Jesus use stories because He had not graduated from "Torah school," or because He was only a carpenter? ... No! Of course not. Perhaps then, because the people of Jesus' day were not very literate, maybe only 11 percent at the most, Jesus was forced to speak in stories so that the uneducated could understand? Maybe ... But wait. How did Jesus speak to the Pharisees? Did He ever use stories? ... Yes, He did. And they understood the message—and some even believed.

We must ask ourselves, could Jesus have given the most stunning lectures, using the most impressive vocabulary in existence? ... Yes, He could have. But Jesus chose words that the common working people of His day could understand, not just the words that would be understood by the most educated people in His day.

Jesus did not come to teach us history; He brought a spiritual message that all who "listened" could comprehend. In STS, attendees learn how to find the spiritual information (treasures) that the stories contain, and then how to form and ask questions in a discussion format that will lead listeners to those treasures.

Anyone following the guidelines of STS, as in found this handbook or learned in an STS workshop, can be an effective practitioner. May the Lord bless His Word as it goes out through these practitioners.

With added information, practice and oversight, practitioners can become provisional instructors. In time, the provisional instructors can move on to becoming certified STS instructors. This book will show how this all comes about. We love watching this multiplication of leaders take place.

What Are Bible Treasures? *The Path*

Once there was a man who left his village and went to the city to work. In the many years he was in the city, the man earned a lot of money. Finally, he returned home, whereupon everyone greeted him as a great friend.

This newly wealthy man wanted to use some of his money to give gifts to his true friends. So he thought of a plan: he left his village for a day and then came back. Then he called everyone together who was saying, "I am your friend," and he asked them all to come meet him at the other side of the nearby hill.

The wealthy man gathered the people who came and then made an announcement. He said, "I've been working on the path that goes to the river. If you follow the path, you will find some treasures. Now go. Find my gifts for you."

So the people left and started walking down the path. A few people went a short ways. "Hmm," they said. "This is an interesting path. Let's look into this." So they stooped down and picked up some sand from the path and took it home to analyze.

Others ran down the path toward the river. When they reached the end of the path, they complained, "We know this path well. There is nothing new. We didn't see any treasures."

The rest of the people continued walking down the familiar path. As they moved along, they began talking with each other, saying things like, "Look at this old fallen tree. Our friend moved it out of the way to make our walk on the path easier." Other walkers noticed that the thorn bushes had been cut back to make the way safer.

Instead of running down the path looking for gifts, these people began walking even more slowly. They wanted to enjoy the results of the hard work that their wealthy friend had done for them. They recognized that the path itself was a gift from their friend.

Suddenly, one walker stopped and called everyone over to look. "Look by the side of the path here, under this bush. There are bags of rice!"

Then another walker called out, "Look over here, under the bushes beside the path! I found a lot of brand new cooking pots!"

Again and again the slow walkers kept discovering hidden treasures just off to the side of the path. They realized that these gifts had been placed there for them by their rich friend. This wealthy man knew that his true friends would trust him and appreciate his path, so they would be the ones to discover the gifts he had placed there for them.

Those who had rushed down the path, that had been lovingly prepared by the rich man, missed all of the treasures. They did not go slowly enough to be able to appreciate the path, or the path maker. (Those who decided to analyze the sand on the path—they are still analyzing. They still have not yet traveled the path!)

Every story in the Bible is a path prepared for us by God. Those who will walk slowly through the path of a Bible story can discover hidden treasures, gifts of truth from God. This we do in *Simply The Story*.

Following Nathan's Example

In 2 Samuel 12:1-14, God uses a certain style of communicating spiritual truth. King David, a faithful man whom God had selected to be the king, had later greatly sinned by committing adultery and then ordering his military leader to murder the woman's husband! Afterward, David tried to hide his sin. So, Nathan the Prophet came to David and told a story:

> There were two men, one rich, one poor. The very wealthy man owned much cattle and sheep. One day when this rich man had company, he stole the one pet lamb that the poor man owned and killed it, and gave it to his guest as a meal!

When David heard Nathan's story, David became extremely angry. In the Bible story David says to Nathan, "As the LORD lives, the man that has done this thing shall surely die! And he must replace the lamb with four lambs, because he did this thing, and because he had no pity."

Then Nathan said to David, "You are the man."

Before David heard Nathan's story, would David, a man who was a follower of God, know that adultery, treachery and murder are wrong? ... Yes! So did David know that he had committed sin? ... Yes. Had David admitted to his sin? ... Correct. He had not faced his sin.

Normally, how would you expect a prophet of God to preach a sermon against adultery and murder? ... What kind of sermon did Nathan use? ... Right. Instead of confronting David directly, Nathan told a story.

Notice what happened. How did David respond? ... Yes. David rightly judged the wealthy man as guilty and even said that the wealthy man should do what kind of replacement? ... And was worthy of what? ... Correct. David said the wealthy man owed four lambs for the one he had stolen, and the man should die!

David felt the story—saw the sin of the wealthy man—and then made a righteous spiritual observation.

After David committed verbally to what was right, Nathan took David into the story and made a spiritual application to David, "You are that man, David." Nathan adds details of how David had sinned against God.

Then, "David said to Nathan, 'I have sinned against the LORD.'" We see later in that story that the punishment of death (which David had told Nathan should come on the wealthy man) instead came to David's own household.

That Bible story about David illustrates the major distinctives of *Simply The Story*, its central parts. After people hear a Bible story and really feel it, they tend to be able to insightfully discuss it. From looking inside the story, they discover and verbally commit to spiritual information about those in the story. We call those discoveries "Spiritual Observations."

After listeners speak aloud in a time of discussion, and share what they see about the characters in the story, the storyteller then invites people to put themselves into the story. They enter into the story personally and consider how today people might encounter similar challenges and opportunities. The storyteller asks questions to encourage the listeners to think about what they observed and how those observations might apply to their own lives today.

Interestingly, we have found that during the discussion of Spiritual Observations, the Holy Spirit oftentimes has already been speaking to listeners on a personal level. In STS, we call these personalized truths "Spiritual Applications."

What or Who Makes This Work?

No matter how many years someone has known the Lord in a personal way, or how much formal or informal Bible education a person may have, there is only one way that the Bible can be understood. Our relationship with God is spiritual. Scripture contains God's spiritual messages to mankind, so the spiritual truths that the Bible contains can only be understood through the teaching of the Holy Spirit.

Far too many believers in Jesus Christ have become dependent on others to teach them the Word of God. Church-goers wait for their pastors to tell them spiritual truth. Some studious learners attend Bible school just to learn more. Pastors attend Bible schools and seminaries to learn, and for ongoing inspiration they look in commentaries and attend conferences to find new information. Seminarians and others also study various authors to increase their understanding.

All of these sources have great value, but the best source of understanding God's message is often overlooked! This source is God's gift to us. What is that source? Consider this story:

After more than three years of personal teaching from Jesus, the disciples heard a startling message from Him. Jesus was leaving them! He said to His disciples, "Let not your heart be troubled, neither let it be afraid."

From what Jesus says, can we know what emotion the disciples were feeling? ... Yes. They were afraid. Their wonderful, personal Teacher would no longer be with them. Who would comfort them? Who would teach them? As part of Jesus' last message to the disciples, He assured them that they would not be alone. Jesus promised a resident Teacher. This Teacher would be with each disciple, day and night, seven days a week.

> But the Comforter, which is the Holy Ghost, whom the Father will send in my name, he shall teach you all things, and bring all things to your remembrance, whatsoever I have said unto you. (John 14:26)

> Howbeit when he, the Spirit of truth, is come, he will guide you into all truth: for he shall not speak of himself; but whatsoever he shall hear, that shall he speak: and he will shew you things to come. (John 16:13)

The best source of understanding God's Word is His Holy Spirit—the gift Jesus left with us.

God explains how the Holy Spirit teaches spiritual truth.

> But as it is written, Eye hath not seen, nor ear heard, neither have entered into the heart of man, the things which God hath prepared for them that love him. But God hath revealed them unto us by his Spirit: for the Spirit searcheth all things, yea, the deep things of God. For what man knoweth the things of a man, save the spirit of man which is in him? even so the things of God knoweth no man, but the Spirit of God.

> Now we have received, not the spirit of the world, but the spirit which is of God; that we might know the things that are freely given to us of God. Which things also we speak, not in the words which man's wisdom teacheth, but which the Holy Ghost teacheth; comparing spiritual things with spiritual.

> But the natural man receiveth not the things of the Spirit of God: for they are foolishness unto him: neither can he know

them, because they are spiritually discerned. But he that is spiritual judgeth all things, yet he himself is judged of no man. For who hath known the mind of the Lord, that he may instruct him? But we have the mind of Christ. (1 Corinthians 2:9-16)

For too long the classroom of the Holy Spirit has stayed empty. Let us attend His class, raise our hands and ask questions. As we study each story, we can ask the Lord for wisdom to understand the content and believe that He will give us the answers.

Chapter 3: *Simply The Story* – A One Page Overview

PREPARATION
STS skill involves easily learning a Bible story and discovering the "spiritual treasures" it contains. Also involved is the forming of oral-style questions that will help facilitate discussion about the story.

PRESENTATION
Two phases take place: first telling the story, then discovering treasures.

Phase One. The story is presented three times, allowing the listeners to become totally familiar with the content. The skills needed are the abilities to: tell a story well, encourage volunteers and review the story's content in an interesting manner.

1. **Tell.** The storyteller tells the story. (The first telling helps the listener picture the story and feel its impact.)

2. **Volunteer.** The storyteller asks one volunteer to retell the story or asks listeners to retell it in pairs, one person to the other. (Listeners will pay close attention to the retelling by their peers to see if they get it "right," which helps place the story into the listeners' memories.)

3. **Lead Through.** The storyteller leads all the listeners through the story a third time. On this last retelling, the storyteller engages everyone in the story by using various methods to get a complete and accurate story retold with the listeners' help.

Phase Two. The storyteller leads the listeners to the spiritual treasures. But now, the storyteller no longer asks the learners to retell the story. Instead, before looking for treasures in each new section, the storyteller first repeats the small part of the story to be explored.

1. **Spiritual Observations.** First, through questions, the storyteller encourages listeners to discover spiritual information. (Listeners are invited to take a look at the activities of the characters in the story. Then, in response to questions, listeners share what they are learning spiritually about the people and how God is working with people and events in the story. Those we call "Spiritual Observations.")

2. **Spiritual Applications.** Second, based on the Spiritual Observations that were found, applications are sought for people's lives today. (The storyteller uses questions to lead listeners to discover and share. We call those findings "Spiritual Applications.")

Chapter 4: How to Prepare a Story the *Simply The Story* Way

To teach using STS style requires three skills:

I.   **How to Select, Learn and Tell a Story Well.**

II.   **How to Find Treasures in the Story.**

III.   **How to Frame and Ask Insightful Questions.**

Skill I: How to Select, Learn and Tell a Story Well

As you go through the process of *Simply The Story*, the one guideline to follow above all others is to trust God's Word. Trust that the stories in the Bible are best told in their entirety as God wrote them. When you tell a Bible story, add no information, leave out nothing, and do not preach or explain the story's content while you tell it.

Selection of Bible Stories

In some situations, you may be assigned a specific story or Bible passage by a leader. If, however, you are selecting your own stories, here are several guidelines.

1.   When you only have one (or just a few) opportunities to tell Bible stories to a specific group, pick stories with content that is appropriate for the age of the listeners and one with the length that fits the time available to teach. Pray for the Holy Spirit to guide you to stories that contain the truths the listeners need to hear.

2.   When God gave us the Bible, He had innumerable historical incidents from which to choose. Of course, God in His wisdom selected the perfect ones needed for humankind. Since God created all people, He knew their needs. Likewise, in His omniscience, God knew every culture and belief system that people would ever develop.

    The Bible is supracultural. That is, its content rises above all cultures. We say this to suggest to storytellers that the Lord has something of spiritual value in every story for all people.

    Do not be overly concerned about picking a "wrong" story to tell a group. As you tell your selected story, know that the Holy Spirit will deliver His message to each person present.

3. In STS we do not preselect some stories to use for evangelism and some for discipleship. Consistently, we received evidence from users of STS that the Holy Spirit can and does move through all stories to disciple and bring people to faith in God.

4. If you will be having multiple opportunities to tell stories to the same listeners, it is best to start at the beginning of the Bible. Most Bible stories are built on the information in the stories that preceded them, so, when possible, select and tell stories in chronological order.

5. When telling or recording stories, you can skip some stories if you feel led. However, if you do skip stories, you will probably want to give an introduction to the next story you tell so its connection to the previous story you told is smooth. Even if you do not skip any stories, it's helpful to prepare listeners for the story you are about to tell by giving them a reminder of the previous story you told. Involve others. Let an attendee tell the last story.

6. When a story is long, maybe over 15 verses, you may want to divide it into two separate stories to teach it. This allows listeners to learn and discuss both sections well. Divide it at its natural break, which may not be exactly in the middle on the passage.

    For example, the story of Naaman in 2 Kings 5:1-27 is one amazing story to tell STS style—IF you have 3 hours to cover the discussion! Actually, there are four distinct stories within the Naaman story. The larger story has natural breaks in the following verses: 1-5, 6-14, 15-19, and 20-27.

7. Some stories contain a very long list, maybe of cities or names. If the story is long enough, divide it into two stories at the point the list begins. Then, in the introduction to your second story, mention the list. Perhaps say, "Citizens from 14 different countries came to the gathering." Then start telling the second story right after the list ends.

    By presenting the information this way, you have told two Bible stories that are accurate to the Scripture. For beginning storytellers and learners, dividing stories helps make the stories easier to remember. As storytellers increase their skills, they can always go back and combine the two stories and include all of the names.

Now that you know how to select a story, let us examine some of the ways to learn to tell it.

1. **Pray** for the ability to remember and understand the story and to tell it accurately and with enthusiasm.

2. **Read the Story Through Once OUT LOUD**. (or listen to it being told or read). As you go through, you may want to change some of the wording. Select words for your story that your particular listeners would use to express themselves. For instance, instead of saying "fearful," you might decide to say "afraid" or "scared." You want to speak conversationally. But be extremely careful to keep the content of the story the same as the Bible!

    If you happen to be one of those fortunate people who read and also speak more than one language, you have access to a unique way to learn a story. Read the story out loud in one language, and then repeat the story in the language you will use when telling the story.

    For example, if you can read Hindi and want to tell the story in English, look at the Hindi and speak the story out loud in English. You then won't be trying to recall exact words. Instead you will be remembering content and can more naturally tell the story, as a story. As well, you will more naturally select words that are conversational.

3. **Close Your Bible and Close Your Eyes! Retell the Story OUT LOUD From Memory.** Just do your best to recall as much of the story as you are able. Begin to see the story in your mind as it takes place. As you go, if you falter or forget parts, don't worry; don't stop. Just keep going. You can add the missed information in a later sentence if it comes back to mind. **This is storytelling, not memorization.**

    For instance, if the text says "Jesus took Peter, James and John...," but suddenly you forget all three names, you could just keep going saying, "Jesus took three disciples..." Then, as you continue telling the story, if you remember their names, instead of saying "they" you just say "Peter, James and John..." (Right now, you are just assembling the story. As you go through this process of reading and repeating the story again, you will probably remember to say the names when they appear in the story!)

4. **Read the Story OUT LOUD Another Time.** As you read, you will notice information you may have added or left out. You will probably be surprised at how much of the story you remembered.

    If the story you plan to tell is long (more than 12 to 15 verses), you may want to learn it in two parts. Many stories have several natural sections. You might want to remember your story as two scenes or pictures in your mind. You are not memorizing words; you are **remembering the exact story by following the pictures in your mind.**

5.	**Again, Close Your Bible, Close Your Eyes and Tell the Story OUT LOUD.** Reading aloud blocks out distracting sounds and presses the story into your memory. Closing your eyes as you tell the story allows you to see it. Picture the people and the surroundings in your mind. This time through, as you repeat the story, you will discover that you can recall even more of the story than the first time you told it. Once more, open your Bible to the story and read it **out loud** to see if you added or left out any information. Even small parts need to be correct. Every part of the story, the way God gave it to us, is important.

6.	**Select Your Beginning and Ending Statements**. Establish the path of your story, where you will start your story and how your story will end. Your selected story may be easy to remember, which means it is one straight path, beginning to end.

7.	**Mental Markers.** Very often your story will have some hard spots, junctions that you will miss, unless you make a mental mark on your path. After you repeat that retelling and checking of yourself a few more times, you may discover a few parts that are difficult to remember. If names or any other definite parts of the story were missed several times, that shows you that you need to place a mental marker at that spot in your story.

	a.	For words, names, or details in your story that are hard for you to recall, draw a silly picture in your mind. (Jerry Lucas, known as the "Memory Doctor," popularized this method.)

	For example, if telling the Jonah story, you might have trouble remembering Jonah's father's name, Amittai. Think of a word or words in your language that sounds like that name you are trying to remember. In English, a storyteller could imagine a ridiculous image of a man wearing a baseball mitt for a necktie: A-mitt-tie.

	You will find that the sillier the picture is that you draw in your mind, the easier those hard words are to remember. In whatever language you speak, find a rhyming word or silly image that brings the name or situation to your thoughts.

	b.	Some who teach storytelling do not stress remembering specific names. We do encourage saying the names in your story, even though they are usually the most difficult parts of the story to remember. The Lord knows that most people struggle to remember names. However, since God did choose in many cases to give us the names of the characters and places in a story, we like to include that information when we tell the story.

8. **Tell and Check Until You Can Go Through Accurately**. Repeat these steps until you know the story well. Keep telling the whole story out loud with your eyes closed, until you repeat it accurately.

    Always guard against adding facts to the story, even facts found in some parallel passage of this Bible story! The Lord made the decision to tell some stories in the Bible more than once. Each telling is slightly different. If God chose to keep the stories separate, so will we. Confining our study to one narrative at a time causes us to dig deeply. That focus prompts us to uncover the unique truths found in that particular account. When the parallel stories are investigated at a later time, the way each account fits together will be discovered.

Stepping Into the Unfamiliar

As we acquire new skills, there is a tendency to incorporate only part of what we are learning into the systems we have already found to be valid.

Let me illustrate. Several of our dedicated volunteer staff agreed to listen to a new teaching piece I was writing for *Simply The Story*. Although my intention was to see if one certain segment had clarity, God used this episode to show me a valuable lesson.

To properly understand the segment, they had to know the story, so I asked these two rather shy people to first learn the story. One, a lady, had attended and worked behind the scenes in four STS workshops. The other, a man in his eighties (who works as if he was 20!) had, until this moment, successfully evaded telling a story.

"If you follow the instructions," I explained, "you can learn this ten-verse story in ten minutes." I reminded them of the STS way of learning a story. "Read the story one time through, out loud. As you read, say the story in natural, spoken words. For instance, in this story, instead of saying 'behold,' you might say 'look.' See in your mind's eye what is happening in the story. Immediately after reading it one time, close your eyes and say aloud as much as you remember of the story.

"Your goal is to remember the exact story, not the exact words. Then go back and read it out loud again. You will notice the parts you left out. Close your eyes and again repeat the story out loud. Do this four times."

These cooperative, servant-hearted people repeated the instructions to me. "Read it out loud in natural, spoken words, close my Bible and tell the story," they dutifully repeated.

So they began. They read—silently! Neither uttered a sound out loud. I interrupted their study. "How were you supposed to read this?"

They both responded, "Out loud."

"But I don't hear anything," I inquired.

"Well," the man stated, "I am just reading it to myself."

"But you already said you knew to read out loud. You are such a cooperative person. Why did you not follow the instructions?" I asked.

"I don't know," he puzzled, "I guess I just never do that."

"And you," I turned to the lady, "Did you know you were supposed to read out loud?" "Yes."

"Then I don't understand. Why did you not read out loud?" Sheepishly she explained, "I felt foolish to do that."

We all laughed, especially when we realized that the story is about Zacchaeus, a man who wanted to see Jesus so badly that he did something that might have been considered foolish. As well, one of the other truths in their story was how Zacchaeus totally followed instructions!

Finally, after quite a bit of coaxing, they broke out of their bondages of "I've never done it that way," and "fear of looking foolish." They read their story out loud, closed their eyes and repeated their story as best as they could.

After four times through, I asked them, "Will you tell your story to me now?" Wonderfully, after only ten minutes of reading out loud and repeating, they both told almost perfect stories!

"So," I joked with the eighty-something man, "do you always memorize ten verses in ten minutes?" He just laughed.

The lady burst out, "I could never learn these Bible stories before! I wanted to. I tried, but I just couldn't do it."

"Have you ever followed all of the instructions?" "No," she smiled, "not till now."

We included this incident to encourage you to fully try all the components of STS. Because right now you are reading these words, it is clear that you are literate. But, since the learning and communication style of STS is oral, to fully do the STS process, you are being asked to step into another world.

By faith, try all of the STS steps as they are laid out. That office incident is quite common, and it shows that using only part of the STS guidelines will not give you the desired end result. AFTER you try STS as outlined, the Lord will probably show you many useful innovations that will enhance your study and STS presentations.

Adding Depth and Listening Interest to the Story

1. **Think About the Context (Setting) of the Story.** Read or listen to the Scripture that leads into your story. Often knowing what occurred in the Bible just before your story (both historically and spiritually) will give you added understanding of your story. After you complete the preparation of your story, you will need to decide if your story needs an introduction or "set up" to help your listeners better understand the story. Later in the book, we will look at how to prepare an introduction.

2. **Avoid Pronouns!!!!!** Listeners will be able to follow the story better, if you use the names of people in the story and specific locations or the names of objects instead of saying "it," "he," "she" or "they." Do this when possible (and as acceptable within a language).

3. **Think About the Timing of the Story.** (The "Timing of the Story" and the next point "Live the Story," are central both to understanding the story and to being able to tell it well.)

   a. We can all read through a Bible story much more quickly than the actual amount of time it took for the story to take place. So, to fully understand a story, read through it slowly. Remember the Path story? Those who went slowly found the treasures.

   b. Picture in your mind each section of the story. Allow the information given in the story to help you step into the story. Consider carefully what the story reveals about what each character is thinking and feeling.

   c. Note that even though the stories in the Bible occurred thousands of years ago, the people in the stories were living those events for the first time. Although we may be familiar with the story we are learning, take note of this. No one in the story had ever lived the incident before it occurred. So walk through the events in your mind as the characters in the story must have experienced them.

4. **Live the Story.** Notice what each character does and says and how each reacts to the other characters in the story. As we "listen" carefully, the actions and words of people tell us much about them

spiritually. Through careful observation, storytellers can understand a story well, enabling them to most accurately tell the story with valid expressions and actions.

Do remind yourself that all of the people we read about in the Bible, even the leaders and prophets of God, are just people. Although many obey God and show faith in hard situations, in every instance each person had to make that choice to believe and trust.

5. **Speak All the Quotes in Your Story.** If the emotion of the speaker is stated in the story, or is very obvious, then use that emotion. Look for anger, sadness, fear, disappointment, etc. Be as dramatic as possible as you speak the words that the character said. If the emotion is not stated, you still can express the words as you think the people (or characters) would have spoken them. But you must make certain what you "think" is justified within the story. Expressing emotion as you quote what characters said gives you an opportunity to give great life to the story.

    If you cannot be certain from the story what emotion the speaker is feeling, do not speak with an emotion that you just "think" the speaker had. That would be adding to the story, which God cautions us in the Bible never to do!

    > What thing soever I command you, observe to do it: thou shalt not add thereto, nor diminish from it. (Deuteronomy 12:32)

    > Every word of God is pure: he is a shield unto them that put their trust in him. Add thou not unto his words, lest he reprove thee, and thou be found a liar. (Proverbs 30:5-6)

6. **Express the Story.** As you practice telling the story, your voice needs to reflect the mood and feeling the story contains.

    a. When people first start telling stories, sometimes in an effort to be dramatic, the storytellers begin the story by speaking in an excited voice—but then they continue with that same excited voice throughout the whole story! Speaking excitedly with an emotional voice for too long eventually wears out the audience, causing listeners to lose interest. In real life, no story would be accurately represented by intense excitement throughout.

    b. Actually, some parts of the story might be about sadness, fear, kindness, disappointment or some other emotion that an excited voice would not correctly represent. Vary your voice. Express the story by raising the volume of your voice, or by speaking softly, as long as you can still be heard. Emphasize parts of a story by speaking more slowly, or saying your words more quickly to illustrate a quick action. Fit your voice's excitement level to the story. The various emotions of the story can be shown in the tone and expression of your voice.

c. In every language, when people converse, there are sounds that are not really words, that will naturally slip into their speech. In most cultures, clicks of the tongue indicate an emotion. These sounds will be unique to every language and culture.

It may be that a sigh shows fatigue, or that an expelling of breath indicates frustration. A quick gasp or intake of air may show surprise or fright. Laughter or a catch in one's voice can deliver an emotion. All of those spoken sounds exist. We learn them from those around us as we grow up.

Increase your skills of telling Bible stories naturally and interestingly by listening for cultural sounds as you converse with others. As you notice new sounds, store them in your mind so that you can purposely use them when you tell Bible stories.

d. Even a pause or a hesitation between words can add great drama and listening interest to the telling of a story. For example, in the story of the one leper the narrator says, "Jesus reached out His hand and touched the leper." If the storyteller speaks those words with no hesitation, a great opportunity is lost.

For Jesus to actually touch a leper is astounding; it shows such great compassion. The storyteller needs to slowly say the words with hesitations in between each movement [by the storyteller] of reaching down to touch the leper. The beautiful moment between Jesus and the leper is seen and heard and felt when the storyteller says in an increasingly slower and increasingly more amazed voice, "Jesus—reached out His hand——and—— touched—the leper."

e. Look for moments of drama within a story. When a healing takes place, or there is anything unusual, or even a strong statement is made by a character inside a story, consider using a hesitation or pause in speech. By doing this, you allow the dramatic incident enough time to unfold and be felt by the listeners.

f. Most stories have some ordinary narration that connects the words of the speakers. Those parts can best be told with a normal voice.

g. Sometimes, however, even the words of the narrator can add interest to a story. The narrator's words can show a change of location or draw attention to an amazing part of the story. These words are spoken with a deep feeling of interest. It is as if the narrator is sharing some secret, exciting information with listeners, so the words are spoken in a loud whisper-like style.

Speaking this way points people to the words that will follow as particularly interesting. Even seemingly ordinary words such as "meanwhile" or "at the same time" or "after they arrived" can be spoken to create interest. You can hesitate and use a tone of voice and body action that hints at some type of intrigue.

7. **Use Actions, Show the Story.** Actions that correctly fit the story can show fear, greed, aggression, flight, surprise, bravery, wisdom, depression and other emotions. Emotions can be demonstrated through even slight gestures. By where you stand, look or gesture, you can establish the location of people, crowds, or places mentioned in your story.

As you speak a person's words, slightly reposition your body to be in the place and looking in the correct direction that simulates where the person is located, where he would have been looking or what the person was doing. For instance, healed people may look amazed and slowly move their newly healed body, or they may become excited and jump for joy. Hesitations in speech and also in movement add realism and drama to storytelling.

A Word of Caution. If you find that those you tell the story to approach you afterwards and say, "You're a great storyteller," or "I love your acting ability"—rethink your presentation. Storytellers are not the feature; God's Word is the feature. Too much dramatic movement by a storyteller can take focus away from the spoken words; people begin to watch more than listen. It is best to make small movements that just illustrate the words you speak. What you want people to say is, "That story spoke to me," or "I am that person in the story."

8. **Stand or Sit to Tell a Story?** In many cultures and situations it is more appropriate for a storyteller to sit down with the people to tell a story than to stand. We suggest practicing your story standing up. That enables you to tell the story with total body actions and positioning. Then, when you have the opportunity to tell a story to a large group or in some other settings, when standing would be the

best way to tell the story, you will have practiced all of the larger actions.

We want listeners to understand and remember the stories we tell them. Not only do actions and expressions contribute to people's interest in the story, they improve people's ability to understand and remember the story's content. Of course, when telling a story seated is the best choice, by all means sit. But even when most of your ministry storytelling is done while seated, you will still be able to use some of the actions that you practiced.

9. **Beginning the Story.** As stated before, when you begin telling the story say, "Now this is the story" or "This is the Bible story." As you start telling the story, hold an open Bible and look at it for a moment as if you are reading it. This indicates to the listener that what you are saying comes out of the Bible. If your story has an introduction, keep your Bible closed while you introduce the story. An introduction is your words—not the story.

When telling some stories you may want to use both of your hands to add drama to your storytelling. As you are speaking, gently set your open Bible on a nearby table or respectful platform. Keep talking as you set it down, so that the listeners will know that you are still telling a story found in the Bible. As you near the end of your story, continue telling your story as you reach over and pick up your open Bible.

(If you are storytelling in a region that is anti-Christian, you may not want to hold a Bible or even tell listeners it is a Bible story. In this case, just tell your story and let the listeners be touched spiritually by the content and the discussion afterwards.)

10. **Look At Everyone Sometimes!** In STS we teach attendees to look at everyone as they tell their story. Interestingly, in one workshop when a new storyteller in a group looked only at me the whole time, a discovery was made. Before correcting him, I asked the man if in his culture, it was expected that he tell his information only to the older or most important person in a group. He answered, "This is true."

Oh no! Culture clash. Our desire in STS is to draw out everyone and encourage all present to become involved in responding to questions. That evening we discussed this cultural conflict at length with the indigenous STS instructors. We concurred that, although respect for elders and leaders is important, no one should be overlooked.

We agreed that storytellers must begin by acknowledging the elders. But, as much as possible, storytellers need to speak to everyone, regardless of the listeners' rank or status in the community. Throughout the presentation, the storyteller continues to include and speak to the high ranking people. But, by also looking at and speaking to others in the group, the storyteller demonstrates (as in the parable of the Good Samaritan) who our neighbors are today.

The god of this world has woven into all of mankind's cultures the mind set to elevate the strong and devalue the weak. Plainly in Scripture, there is a biblical principle of including everyone. Jesus did this. He was often criticized for this very act of noticing and spending time with those His culture considered the lower sort of people.

In STS workshops, we show how to purposely involve those people who most societies push aside: women, children, the simple, outcasts, the uneducated and ethnic groups deemed as worthless.

When something in a culture clashes with Scripture, believers must make a choice:

> **Whether to let one's culture guide one's actions and beliefs, or to let the Word of God move one's actions and beliefs to a higher level—each believer must decide.**

11. **End the Story.** When you complete the story, tell the listeners, "This is the end of the story," and close your Bible.

12. **Tell Your Selected Story Often**, to anyone who will listen to it, until it flows easily. If no people are available, tell it to a nearby animal or a tree. Remember, you are not memorizing exact words, but you are telling an exact story.

Be Bold – Be Trusting – No Writing!

Can you imagine Jesus standing up to deliver the Sermon on the Mount and first setting His notes on a lectern in front of Him? Probably not. When someone asks you to tell your testimony, or how you met your spouse, or the happiest experience of your life, do you refer to your notes to answer? Some types of information we experience—so we remember it. We own it. Even when we talk with a friend about our day, we tell it by memory. We own the information, and because it is a story, we can easily repeat it.

We know STS requires you to acquire new skills. In the past, if you have ever been a speaker or teacher, you no doubt used notes to recall your presentation. When you lecture or learn new material for yourself that is wrapped in topical content, notes are needed. But with a story, you don't need notes.

If you tasted some homemade chocolate cake and found it delicious, you might ask for the recipe, the mix of ingredients. But if you went home to make a cake like that for yourself, would it make sense to swap vanilla for chocolate and rice for flour? ... No. Of course not. The uniqueness of the cake is based on the recipe.

We suggest following the STS "recipe," trusting that each step of STS has a purpose.

When a story is prepared for STS delivery, it should all be done in your mind, no notes! For those who read a lot, this does not seem possible. As we mentioned, almost everyone who reads has learned to depend on written notes to recall information. But you do not need notes in the STS process, so we ask you to do something very unusual. Study and prepare a lesson and write NOTHING! Yes, we are serious—NO written notes.

Let us encourage you to attend one of the *Simply The Story* workshops. There you will experience learning a ten-verse Bible story in ten minutes. As well, STS instructors give individualized help in learning how to discover spiritual treasures and prepare questions. ALL this you would do without any written notes!

Skill II: How to Find Treasures in the Story

The second skill you need to acquire is how to find the treasures within the story that you plan to tell.

What are treasures in a Bible story? We call the spiritual truths that God weaves into every Bible story "treasures." These treasures are the combination of Spiritual Observations and Spiritual Applications.

The Spiritual Observations are the ways God worked in the lives of people in the story.

The Spiritual Applications are the spiritual truths, based on those observations, that apply to our lives today.

Helping Seekers Find. Remember the story of Philip and the Eunuch in Acts. We discover there an important man, an Ethiopian eunuch, who sat in his chariot reading in the book of Isaiah. The Lord sent Philip to the eunuch to explain the Scriptures. Hearing a story is good, but helping people understand the content of the story they just heard has a biblical precedent.

How to Find the Treasures Called "Spiritual Observations"

You are not just investigating the story as a piece of history; you are also seeking to discover what is happening spiritually. God always has a plan for everyone in each Bible story. From what those characters in the story learn (or don't learn), we can discover what God wants us to learn. As explained earlier, part of the way you remember and understand a Bible story is to live that story.

As you live a story through what each character says and does, notice also how God works in the story. This "living in the story" helps you to discover some of the story's treasures.

To find these spiritual treasures, go through the story and take some time to look at what is said about each individual or group of people in the story. God will be working with everyone in the story to teach them something.

If you have printed or audio Scripture available that contains passages of the Bible that precede your story, it is important to investigate that information. Consider what comes just before your story. Is there anything that might help you understand who the characters in your story are, what they know, and what they have experienced?

Short Overview of Finding Spiritual Observations:
The Wise Counsellor

Some villagers had been disputing over a well and water rights for a long time, so they went to a wise counsellor to get advice. This counsellor was known to ask many questions, because he wanted to thoroughly understand the problem so that he could give good advice.

So, the counsellor first asked, "Can you briefly explain the situation? In just a few words, what is troubling you?"

After the villagers told the counsellor their short version of the dispute, he then wisely asked, "Did anything happen before this problem started that could help me better understand it?" After the villagers told what led to the dispute, the counsellor said, "Now tell me the whole story, but please tell it slowly." So the people began to tell their story.

As soon as the villagers told part of their story, the counsellor stopped them and asked, "Now tell me, at this point in your dispute, did any of you say anything or maybe did you do something, because that will help me to better understand what happened?"

After the villagers replied, the counsellor also asked, "At that time, did any of you make any choices? And if you made a choice—were there any other choices you could have made?" Whenever a choice was mentioned, the counsellor would ask, "And did you see any results from that choice and who else might have been impacted?"

So the counsellor continued in this manner. He would say to the villagers, "Please tell more of your story." Then, after they told a little more, he would say, "Do stop there," and he would ask the same questions about what the villagers may have said and done, choices they made or could have made, and the results and long-range impact of their choices.

Finally they finished telling their story. Then, because the wise counsellor had listened carefully to the villagers' answers, he truly understood this dispute and was able to give them good advice.

In *Simply The Story*, we want to discover the valuable information that every Bible story contains. To locate this treasure, we ask questions, much the same as the questions that the wise counsellor asked. But we go deeper than just what happened in the story, which is only history. We want to see what we can learn spiritually.

Remember how that wise counsellor first asked the villagers to "briefly explain the situation"? Most Bible stories and passages also have some kind of tension or problem in them. We call that the "situation." Before we begin to go slowly through the Bible story and ask questions, we first look for its situation. *Are those in the story hungry or in danger? Are they scared or confused or maybe having some kind of disagreement?*

Knowing that situation causes the people in the story to become real to us. We are emotionally drawn into the story as we realize what it must be like for people to experience that kind of situation.

Also, before the villagers were allowed to tell their story, that counsellor asked the villagers to tell what happened before they experienced their problem. In the same way, when looking for treasures inside a Bible story, we look for the setting, also called the context.

But Notice This. Although the historical context of a Bible story is helpful, we go beyond that, beyond what the wise counsellor did. We also look for the spiritual context. We look for ways God may have been working in these people's lives. We might try to find how they had gotten into their situation, or how long they had been struggling, or if they had been serving God. Finding the spiritual setting or context will help us better understand the spiritual content of the story we are exploring.

Remember how the wise counsellor had asked the villagers to tell their story slowly, and how in each part he asked what the villagers said and did? In *Simply The Story*, we start at the beginning of the story and slowly and carefully listen to each section as we saw it happen in our minds when we learned it. We ask ourselves—*What might we learn spiritually from the actions and words of each person in this part of the Bible story?*

We consider everyone mentioned in that section, including Jesus and God the Father. We ask, "What could I learn spiritually from what was said and done, from the choices that were made (or could have been made), and from the direct results of the choices and all who were impacted?" The answers to all of these questions reveal what we call "Spiritual Observations."

This slow and careful hunt for treasure allows us to see what living people, like ourselves, said and did in real-life encounters. We learn a great deal when we consider the results and impacts of the choices they made—or could have made.

And beyond what the wise counsellor asked, when looking at Bible stories, we look for God, even when God's name is not mentioned in a Bible story. We always look for how God was working in the situation and in people's lives, and for what we can learn about Him.

Real People Once Lived the Bible Stories

Begin to think about the living, breathing people who actually experienced this situation. Realize that they had feelings and emotions, such as you have. Imagine how people in a circumstance like this "might" have felt at that moment, which is not necessarily what they "should" feel. Then, to learn more about the story, look at the different characters in it, one section at a time, as the story takes place.

Look at the first part of the story and carefully observe and listen. Ask yourself: *What can I learn about the people spiritually from what I see them do and hear them say? Do they seem brave or afraid, or sad or happy, or do I see some other emotion? Can I see what is causing them to feel and act that way?*

Look in each section for choices. Maybe the person could have made a different choice? Realize that in every story in the Bible, everyone, including God the Father and Jesus, had many options or choices they could have made.

When you start seeing all the different possible choices characters could have made, you discover truth. Recognize that these choices were first made in their minds, then they acted upon those choices. In the story you are investigating, you only see the choice that was made.

Start thinking: *What other choices might have been made that may have been better, or perhaps, not as wise?*

Maybe the choice was a poor choice, and you see that the results are negative or hurtful because of the choices made. Maybe it was a good choice and something positive happened. Possibly something surprising occurred. Maybe something first looked like a bad result, but then it turned out well. You need to wonder. *Who else was being impacted in that part of the story because of the choice that was made, and how were they impacted?*

Ask yourself: *How do I see God in this story? What do I learn about Him from what He says and does?*

So, that is what we do to discover Spiritual Observations. We go to each section in the story and ask those same kinds of questions. We look at words, actions, and choices made (or ones that could have been made) and notice the results and the impact of those choices on others. And then always we ask: *What did I see God doing or allowing in those people's lives?*

As you explore every story, looking for spiritual treasures, some of the variations of the *Wise Counsellor* questions could be:

- *What did each character in the story do and say?*

- *What does this show me about that person spiritually?*

- *Can I know from the story if the person is a believer, a seeker, a doubter or a rejecter?*

- *Was faith or doubt being shown?*

- *How did God use circumstances in the story to warn, teach or encourage?*

For those who like detailed information, what follows are sample questions you might use to find spiritual treasures. These are just suggestions to give you an idea of how many different ways you can look for the wealth of treasures that might be found in a story.

Ask Yourself:

- *Is there anything in the story that surprised me: actions of God or people, or the results of people's behavior?* As you carefully "listen" to the story the way God presents it to us in the Bible, see if you can discover the reason for the surprising part.

- *What came before this incident that could give me some insight as to who the characters are and why they behave as they do?*

- *Do I see any of the characteristics of God demonstrated, such as patience, longsuffering, anger, knowledge, justice, kindness, grace, mercy, concern for the weak, equal respect for all people or love?*

- *To whom did God show those characteristics and does that teach me anything?*

- *Can I know from the story if the individuals in it are believers or unbelievers?*

- *Does it look like the people in the story are sincere seekers, skeptics or hardened rejecters of God?*

- *Does anyone in the story have a problem? If so, how big is the problem?*

- *How does the person with a problem try to handle the difficulty?*

- *If the person with a problem goes to God for help, how does that person ask for the help?*

- *Does the person approach God with respect or arrogance?*

- *How does God respond to this approach, and what might that show us?*

- *Is there a leader in the story who follows God, and if so, what are the results of the obedience?*

- *Is there a leader in the story who does not follow God, and if so, what are the results of the disobedience?*

- *Does anyone in the story change beliefs or attitudes?*

- *Do any of the characters show evidence of faith, love, mercy, anger, fear, hope, prejudice, doubt, greed, confusion, ignorance, wisdom, respect, disrespect, superstition or other attitudes?*

- *How does God respond to those people's beliefs, feelings, words or actions, and what does God's response show us?*

- *Do some characters in the story change their behavior?*

- *What exactly causes them to change?*

- *What happens when they do change and what might that teach us?*

- *Are there any miracles or supernatural events in the story, and if so, how did they affect the people in the story?*

How to Find the Treasures Called "Spiritual Applications"

Finding Spiritual Applications. After we have looked carefully at a story, we want to know what this story could mean to us today. This is the time we look for "Spiritual Applications." We can do this by placing ourselves into the story that we just carefully observed. We looked at the story through the eyes of those who lived it. Next, from inside the story, one section at a time, we visit each of the Spiritual Observations that were discovered.

Key to STS Success – Spiritual Applications need to be based on the **Spiritual Observations** that you discover in a story.

Ask yourself these questions:

1. *Hmm?…That situation that I observed in the story…Today, does anything like that happen?*

2. *If so, in what ways does something similar to that happen?*

3. *Has that ever happened to me—or to anyone I know?*

4. *Is it happening right now and if so, how is it happening and how can what is in this story help?*

Try using some of the same questions that helped you find the spiritual observations to find specific personal applications. Maybe ask these:

- *Yes. That happened to me before. What did I say? What did I do?*

- *Did I have any choices, and what choice did I make?*

- *What could I have done? What was the result of my choice?*

- *Who all was impacted by my choice, and in what way were they impacted?*

- *If I am going through something like this right now, how am I reacting? What did I learn from what happened in the story that helps me to know what I should do in my circumstance?*

Lastly, in the story, ask yourself:

- *How do I see God working in my situation, or in the life of someone I know who is in this position?*

- *What did I learn, or what should I have learned about God and about His character?*

When you first read through a story, its content sometimes can be confusing. You may wonder why God responds as He does to a person in the story. Sometimes when you read a story, you may think to yourself,

"This is a nice story, but I do not observe anything spiritual in it. And I sure do not see how this relates to my life!"

Look for this. Every story in the Bible contains something for us today. See if you can discover what the following two Scriptures tell us about the usefulness of all of the information God put in the Bible. This insight will encourage you to try to find out why God acts as He does in a story and to know that there are Spiritual Observations and Applications to be seen in every Bible story.

> All scripture is given by inspiration of God, and is profitable for doctrine, for reproof, for correction, for instruction in righteousness: That the man of God may be perfect, throughly furnished unto all good works. (2 Timothy 3:16-17)

> Now all these things happened unto them for ensamples: and they are written for our admonition, upon whom the ends of the world are come. Wherefore let him that thinketh he standeth take heed lest he fall. There hath no temptation taken you but such as is common to man: but God *is* faithful, who will not suffer you to be tempted above that ye are able; but will with the temptation also make a way to escape, that ye may be able to bear it. (1 Corinthians 10:11-13)

These verses say that all of the words in the Bible, including the words in the stories, are written to us—and for us. Since we know God does not just put words in a story to make the pages come out even, then we need to begin to carefully look at Bible stories to find out what all of the information in a story should mean to us.

As the storyteller and the designer of questions, there are steps you will take to help your listeners discover those truths for themselves.

You cannot lead listeners to the treasures in the story until you first discover them for yourself!

If, while preparing a story, you as a storyteller are not impacted spiritually by the story, it is a good time to go back and seek God for the truths you may have missed. If you have followed all of the guidelines for finding treasures and you have not yet found any spiritual truths in that story, you are not yet equipped to tell it to others.

Once you go through the story and do discover some of its many lessons (treasures), you are now ready to design questions that can gently lead listeners to discover those treasures for themselves.

The Importance of Asking Questions

If you were out walking and discovered a treasure, you would be thrilled! If you took that treasure back and shared it with your friends, they would be very happy to receive it. But their happiness upon receiving it would not be as great as yours when you discovered it. Discovery is a thrill in itself.

Use easy-to-answer questions during the beginning of discussion-style teaching. **This is vital to the success of the STS Bible study concept.**

Many people do not know that there is a wealth of spiritual truths in the Bible. Others know that there are many spiritual treasures in Bible stories, but they do not realize that they are capable of finding those treasures. When people discover even simple information, and they receive approval, they are encouraged to look for more answers.

Most believers are not accustomed to carefully looking at the words and meanings in a Bible story. Purposeful questions (even if they are yes/no questions) are useful to move people toward discovering spiritual observations for themselves.

In STS, as we begin working with a new group of learners, we often lead them right up to a treasure and almost hand it to them. The skilled teacher can imperceptibly lead responders so that they think that they did most of the discovering! When class members are able to uncover even a small part of a treasure for themselves, they are encouraged to continue to look for more treasures.

Those with advanced Bible school or seminary education may have learned how to dissect or analyze the story, but may not have developed the skill of listening to a story as a whole. As we have said, STS keeps the Bible story together and the story is listened to and heard as a stand-alone container of truth.

Stepping in a Hole. Occasionally you meet people (who may or may not have religious education) who they think that they just about know all that can be known about the Bible! To help them, you can use a question that allows these proud people to voluntarily step into a hole. The "hole" is a faulty misconception or false assumption that is not substantiated by the story. So you use a question that does not give away the answer, a question you know will allow poor listeners to offer their incorrect information. You might respond, "Hmm, that is interesting," and then move on.

As the discussion continues, and the correct answer becomes obvious, those quick responders realize that they made a mistake. You have not corrected them, but the mistake they made gently reveals the fact that they do not know as much as they first thought. That surprising experience of falling into that subtle trap encourages self-satisfied participants to become more interested in truly listening and learning.

At times, people discover that what they had previously heard about the story (and had just assumed was accurate) is not valid, and that they had missed a lot about the story. These people come to recognize that they must take more responsibility and listen well to the story to see what is truly there.

The Holy Spirit – The Great Teacher

As believers, when we encounter the unsaved, do we only quote John 3:16 to them and then not talk with that person about the verse afterwards? ... Do we refrain from discussing that Scripture because we think it is only the Holy Spirit's job to teach? ... No! If at all possible—we discuss that verse.

We know the Bible says that the Holy Spirit will guide us into all truth. But as we travel the world sharing STS, we continually find, to our sadness, that most believers do not even KNOW that there are treasures in Bible stories, let alone know that God will help them to learn!

So, still the Holy Spirit waits to teach, standing in front of an empty classroom.

In STS, when we prepare a story, we ask the Lord to show us treasures in the story, and we seek His help to form questions that will help us lead others to the treasures we have found. As we ask listeners the questions, we pray that the Holy Spirit will guide the discussion. Then, as discovery by the listeners is made, we recognize that the Holy Spirit is speaking to every heart in the room, including ours.

Occasionally, questions will come from your listeners that must be answered from other stories and information in the Bible. If you know the answer and can give a biblical source, you need to seek God for wisdom on whether to give a complete answer then, or to just give a short overview response. Or, you may be led to just say, "Good question. Let's wait as that is a whole new direction. Another time I plan to tell a whole Bible story that deals with your excellent question."

Stay sensitive to the listeners. The Holy Spirit, or a person's spiritual hunger, may be prompting that unexpected question. Pray to know if an out-of-the-story question might be a God-led opportunity for truth to be discovered right then. Don't miss that chance. Answer that question!

Storytellers using STS discussion format gradually learn the skill of asking high-quality questions. As the people begin to find their own treasures, wise leaders learn that they can back away from giving obvious clues and slowly allow the responders to do more and more of the discovering. The thrill is watching the awakening of God's gift to do discovery thinking.

Show Love

When we use this discussion-style method, we must all use the one vital key to success described in 1 Corinthians 13:1; we must show love. "Though I speak with the tongues of men and of angels, and have not charity, I am become as sounding brass, or a tinkling cymbal."

Know this. Most people are frightened when they have to stand in front of a group and speak, so you need to be very encouraging in your treatment of them.

At times you may be teaching leaders or pastors. Although they are no doubt comfortable in front of people, most of them have not been "corrected" publicly (or at least not for a long, long time!).

So, as you teach using discussion, be particularly sensitive in your responses both to the frightened ones and to the leaders who are not accustomed to public correction. As listeners retell the story, or respond to questions, or even offer their own observations, remember this. No matter how poorly people may respond, it is essential that the storyteller/teacher be very gentle and affirming in the way corrections are made.

Always remember that gentle corrections said with a smile can be received more easily than stern corrections. Keep in mind that you as the storyteller set the group's atmosphere. You have a choice. You can either give the listeners a feeling of investigation and discovery by encouraging them to submit their ideas and thoughts or—you can create tension and discourage participation by making the participants feel as if the whole discussion time is an exam and they must always give the "correct" answer.

Again, as you work hard to remember your story and ask your questions, think of the people you are leading. Respond to them, keeping uppermost in your mind that it is not your skill that matters most; it is the love shown to the people as you use your skills!

Skill III: How to Frame Your Questions

The major goals and fruit of telling Bible stories and then discussing them afterwards, are these:

- Learning the character of God.

- Learning what He wants for and from mankind.

- Seeing and admitting the truth about ourselves.

After an STS workshop in Kenya, a church planter who attended shared a wise observation. This man, strong in theological training, let go of his city business to minister, but in four years he had seen little fruit in his rural village work.

To come to this workshop he traveled two days by camel, one day by "airbus" (hitching a ride on the top of a passing truck) and one day by bus! He loved what he learned in the workshop and felt empowered! He stated, "I have been teaching what others taught me, but until this training I did not know how to learn from the Bible.

**"I now see that I cannot take people
to a place where I have not yet been."**

This is why we use questions. First the storytellers learn new information for themselves from God's Word, and then, through questions, the storytellers lead others to the valuable truths they have learned.

Leading with "bread crumbs" is a skill we teach in STS workshops. People starting out learning STS often try to ask the one "perfect" question to lead people to a treasure. This rarely works. To coax a bird into a cage, you can't just drop a loaf of bread in front of the cage and expect the bird to find the cage. Instead, you lay a trail of many small bread crumbs to lead it into the cage. In the same way, when you use questions to lead people to discover a spiritual treasure, most often you need to ask a series of small questions that will easily invite and allow listeners to discover.

Please note. Coming next is a practice story of *Abram and Sarai.* In it, and in several other stories that appear later in this handbook, many Spiritual Observations, Applications and questions are written for you. But in STS, we teach you to NEVER write your questions! You don't need to and it hampers interaction. We list questions in a written form in this handbook only so that those who are literate, and who may not be able to learn STS by attending a hands-on workshop, will be able to mentally walk through the preparation process of STS. These are only sample questions. In time for your own study and for teaching others, you will gain the skill of thinking in questions.

As you, the storyteller, move through the stories, some of the observations and applications that we list will be discovered and offered by those you teach even before you arrive at the questions that are supposed to lead them to those treasures! This early finding of treasures by learners is desirable, as it shows that people are learning how to look deeply into Scripture and discover treasures for themselves.

Developing Questions to Lead Others to the Treasures

To frame questions that help others discover the treasures you have found, go back to the beginning of the story. Walk through the story in your mind, thinking about the Spiritual Observations you discovered. Remember how the wise counsellor showed the importance of asking many questions in each section of the story? That is how you found your Spiritual Observations.

In the same way, you may need to ask your listeners a series of questions to allow them to discover as you did. In fact, if you take time to recall the questions you asked to find your observations, often you can just reuse the same questions. Ask others those same questions!

For instance, if you were telling the story in Genesis 12:10-20, you would have observed many things as you prepared, even in the first few verses.

> And there was a famine in the land: and Abram went down into Egypt to sojourn there; for the famine was grievous in the land. And it came to pass, when he was come near to enter into Egypt, that he said unto Sarai his wife, Behold now, I know that thou art a fair woman to look upon: Therefore it shall come to pass, when the Egyptians shall see thee, that they shall say, This is his wife: and they will kill me, but they will save thee alive. Say, I pray thee, thou art my sister: that it may be well with me for thy sake; and my soul shall live because of thee. (Genesis 12:10-13)

You probably noticed as you learned the story that, at the beginning, Abram made choices. He could have trusted God, but instead showed fear. He ran from the Promised Land because of a famine, went to Egypt, and asked Sarai to lie to protect him. (Some may see a conflict in observing that going to Egypt was wrong, because in a later incident Jacob and his family were led by God to go to Egypt. But of course, the words "led by God" do show the difference in the two situations.)

After this, and many other discoveries, you would have gone back and formulated some Spiritual Applications that you based on those observations. You might see that God has given all people promises that are based on our going to and staying in the place of obedience to the Scriptures. Then you would see the application of how in times of stress, we can make bad judgments and go to the world for help instead of consulting God. As well, you would realize that sometimes in our time of running, we sin even more, maybe by conspiring or lying, or even by involving those who trust us in the sin we are committing!

Now Turn Your Observations Into Questions

Anchor Questions in the Story. As you develop questions to lead your listeners to discover the treasures you have found, anchor your questions in the story.

Here are some questions that could be used to open up a lot of discovery based on the Spiritual Observations just mentioned.

1. *From the story we learned and talked about together the last time, where had God told Abram to go and what did God say that He would do for Abram there?*

2. *We saw that a famine prompted Abram to leave the Promised Land and go to Egypt for help. Can you think of anything else Abram could have done besides leave the land when food was short?*

3. *Can we know from this story what kind of emotions or feelings controlled Abram in this story? Do you see any emotion in Abram from what Abram told Sarai to tell the inhabitants of Egypt? What do you think of that?*

4. *When we talked together about the story before this one, do you remember if God had given Abram any promises that could have helped Abram to be bold and not fearful? If so, what were they? Where does it look to you that Abram put his trust?*

5. *Was anyone close to Abram hurt by his sin? What do you see there?*

Based on the Spiritual Observations that the listeners just discovered through discussion, look at the following sample questions that could open up the discovery of Spiritual Applications.

1. *God gave Abram instructions on a location for blessing. In any stories we have looked at together, did any of them have instructions from God on where we need to live to be blessed? Maybe not. But can we discover any principles on how God wants us to live to be blessed? What might some of those be?*

2. *Today, do followers of God ever face life-threatening situations? What kinds of very difficult situations might they encounter? Have you, or anyone you know, ever been faced with a possibly life-threatening*

situation? Is there anything we saw in Abram's choices that might have helped us make better decisions in our difficult situations?

3. *Abram let his emotions rule and showed a lack of faith. Today does that happen? What does it look like? When people lack faith, who might they run to for help instead of God? What in this story could help us think more carefully in times of possible panic?*

4. *When things looked bad, Abram left the place God had directed him to go. Are there ever any occurrences in people's lives today that could tempt them to leave the place to which God had called them? Has this happened to you or someone you know?*

5. *If hard circumstances come in our lives, could what we saw Abram do give us ideas on what we should do or not do? Such as what?*

6. *Are there ever times today when we let the wrong emotions determine our decisions? What kinds of emotions sometimes rule people when difficulty comes into their lives? Have you or someone you know, ever let emotions move you into making poor decisions? Would you be able to share that experience?*

7. *In any Bible stories that we have discussed together, can you think of any promises God made that people today can trust?*

8. *Remember how Abram's lack of faith affected a lot of people? Today, could our lack of trust in God ever affect others? What might that look like? Has that happened to you or someone you know?*

Those are just a few observation and application questions that you might ask from the first part of that story in Genesis.

Note this. Although you have questions prepared that can lead listeners to treasures you have found, you must always be responsive to the questions, observations and answers of your listeners. They may see other treasures or have questions about the part of the story you are covering. Ask your prepared questions. But if those you lead see different treasures, ones that are in the story, let the discussion go there. Put your questions aside. How beautiful it is to watch the Holy Spirit speak directly to listeners.

How to Form an Introduction for the Story

After you have completed your hunt for spiritual treasures in the story, you are ready to decide if your story needs an introduction. We prepare introductions after we have found all of the observations and applications, because it is not until we have finished studying the story that we know all that needs to be included in the introduction.

The introduction provides the setting and background for the story the listeners are about to hear. It prepares the listeners to receive the story and understand it within the context of what has come before in the Scriptures.

What Goes Into an Introduction?

1. If you need an introduction, at most it should only be a few words or sentences. Introductions are by nature more of a documentary style than a story, so keep introductions short to maintain listeners' interest. Short is also preferable since information received in a documentary style is more difficult to remember than information in a story. Here are three reasons you might use an introduction:

    a. Use an introduction to set up the story if it is needed to place the story in a time or situational context. Make certain your introduction is vital to the understanding of your selected story.

    b. Sometimes a story has terminology in it that would be new or confusing to the listeners. You can define those terms in the introduction before you begin the story. Words or terms that might need defining could be ones such as "Synagogue," "Son of Man," or "Sons of the Prophet."

    c. During the question phase, you may want listeners to discover a treasure in the story that depends on them knowing some piece of Old Testament information. For instance, you might be telling the story in John chapter one where John says, "Behold the Lamb of God which takes away the sin of the world." So, in the introduction you might mention that many times in the Bible God instructed His followers to bring a lamb for sacrifice when they had committed a sin.

2. Whatever information you feel your listeners must know to understand the story, or to respond afterwards to questions about the story, needs to be included in your introduction.

3. Keep in mind that sometimes no introduction may be needed.

4. In STS we use only information found in the Bible. We do not use extra-biblical information or Greek/Hebrew word definitions since that kind of information is only available to a select few. We want to encourage and empower all believers to share Scriptures through stories. We need to show learners, by our example, how to find deep truths in the Word—from the Word. Teach them to trust the story.

5. The introduction is Bible information you have compiled. After you finish saying your introduction, make it clear that your introductory set up is done, by saying something such as: "Now this is the story" or "This is the Bible story." (There's no need any more to say, "This story is about…" Instead, let the story tell the people what it is about!)

Chapter 5: Let's Try Our Skills of Preparation and Presentation

First, Learn This Sample Story

You might want to go back and review Skill I and use that information to learn this Bible story in Luke.

> Now it came to pass, as they went, that he entered into a certain village: and a certain woman named Martha received him into her house. And she had a sister called Mary, which also sat at Jesus' feet, and heard his word. But Martha was cumbered about much serving, and came to him, and said, Lord, dost thou not care that my sister hath left me to serve alone? bid her therefore that she help me.
>
> And Jesus answered and said unto her, Martha, Martha, thou art careful and troubled about many things: But one thing is needful: and Mary hath chosen that good part, which shall not be taken away from her. (Luke 10:38-42)

Preparation: Finding Spiritual Treasures

Treasure Hunt 1 – Finding Spiritual Observations

During the time you spent learning the story, you may have seen some valuable treasures. As you now go back and slowly look at the story, one section at a time, use the *Wise Counsellor* questions. You will find even more treasures.

Try each of the *Wise Counsellor* questions: *What is the situation in this story? Is there anything that happened in the Bible before this story (historically or spiritually) that could help me understand the story better? What can I learn spiritually from what people said and did? Were choices made, and if so, what other choices could have been made? Were there any results from those choices and who all might have been impacted?* Use the tools the counsellor used—his many questions. And beyond just what the counsellor asked, we also ask, *Where do we see God at work in this situation and in people's lives?*

All of those questions will help you find Spiritual Observations such as these:

1. When Martha finds herself unable to complete all the serving by herself, she makes some poor decisions. Although she gave the

invitation, Martha blames others for her plight. She accuses Jesus of not caring. She bosses Jesus. She fails to ask Jesus for help.

2. Martha calls Jesus "Lord," but she behaves as if she is the one in charge.

3. Jesus does not give any response to Martha's disrespect.

4. Jesus lovingly corrects Martha.

5. Martha thought what she was doing was necessary, but Jesus said Mary chose the one thing that was necessary.

6. Martha had a choice.

7. Mary chose for Jesus and against her culture and against the expectations that others had for her.

8. Jesus would not let what Mary had chosen be taken from her.

Treasure Hunt 2 – Finding Spiritual Applications

Now, based on the Spiritual Observations that we listed and some you just found, go back into the story and look for some treasures of Spiritual Applications.

First, you recall a Spiritual Observation you found, and then you ask some key questions, such as: *Today does such a thing happen? In what ways can it happen? Has it ever happened to me or someone I know? And, What can I see in the story to help if it ever happens to me?*

Here are some of the Spiritual Applications that those questions might help you discover:

1. Be careful that you do not take on so much work that you lose the vital time you need to learn from God's Word.

2. How sad it is when there is a problem in our lives, to say to God, "Don't you care?" That must break His heart.

3. When we make choices to take on more than we can accomplish, how foolish it is to blame God for not caring about our load!

4. Should we be TELLING God how to solve our problems?

5. Do we ever take on more work than we can accomplish, maybe even doing work for God that He has not directed us to do?

6. So many times we question God's love for us when a situation does not transpire as we think it should.

7. Jesus was patient and longsuffering as he corrected Martha. So often, even when we treat God disrespectfully, He is longsuffering and speaks kindly to us.

8. Just as Jesus' genuine concern and personal relationship with Martha is shown when He calls her by name, so God knows us by name and speaks to us personally.

9. It is not that spending time in the kitchen, or serving, or doing any other ministry work is wrong, but if our work takes us away from hearing God speak through His Word, we have not chosen the good thing.

10. In Jesus' final statement about Martha's behavior, He says that Mary chose the one thing that is necessary. Obviously, by the way Martha wanted Mary to stop what she is doing and come help serve, Martha thinks what she herself is doing is the necessary thing.

    Sometimes we decide what we are doing is the most necessary thing. However, it may not be what God thinks is the one necessary thing for us to do.

11. Sometimes we take charge of situations and don't stop to ask God what He wants us to do. We make the decisions on our own about what is most important and necessary. And we may even decide to pull people away from what God has called them to do!

12. Jesus says that what Mary is doing is the good thing that will not be taken away.

    In the final judgment, as God looks at what we have done in our lives, it may be that some of what we decided to do for God was not the good choice. But if it was the good choice it will not be taken away!

13. Many times we must choose against our culture and family, against what people expect of us, when we choose spiritual options.

Now that you have found the treasures for yourself, it is time for you to go back to the beginning of the story and begin to form questions that will lead the listeners to discover those treasures for themselves. What we're going to do next is look at an STS Presentation that would use some of the questions you might have formed.

So, let's now review what you actually do when you tell a story to real people…

Presentation Phase One:
Telling the Story Three Times

Letting the listeners hear the story three times helps them know the story well enough to respond accurately to the questions:

1. **You tell the story.**

2. **Ask a volunteer to retell the story.**

3. **Lead through the story.** (This is actually you retelling the story, but involving listeners to help you tell it as you go through it.)

First Time – You Tell the Story

Tell the story as accurately and as interestingly as you can. Use lots of body motions and gestures to illustrate the story as you speak.

Second Time – Ask a volunteer to retell the story

The main purpose of asking for volunteers is to encourage people to speak aloud in a group. This volunteer time is the group's first personal involvement in the process. So when a volunteer is treated kindly and is shown respect, then as the presentation continues, not only will that person be more likely to speak aloud and answer questions, but the rest of the group will also have noticed that kind treatment. That kindness will move them closer to feeling safe to speak aloud.

This segment of the STS process is NOT where we expect people to learn the story. Being able to accurately tell the story comes later.

If you have time limitations for the presentation, skip this second telling of the story (the volunteer part) and go straight to the third telling.

There are two ways to call for a volunteer.

Option 1. Say, "Turn to the person next to you, and one of you can retell the story to the other." As mentioned, the biggest value of having volunteers retell the story is that it encourages people to speak aloud. Since most people are hesitant to speak in public, this option is the gentlest way to encourage volunteerism. People usually sit next to someone they know, so nearly everyone will be brave enough to turn to that person, and one will retell the story to the other.

Even in the Christian community most teaching is done lecture style, so to help people expand their ways of learning, we need to provide an environment that helps them speak up and voice their thoughts. When you are telling a story to a group for the first time, this option of asking people to retell the story to someone sitting next to them is **the best way** to ask for a volunteer to retell.

Here is a tip! If you think you may have forgot to tell part of the story, using this first option gives you time to recheck your telling of the story for accuracy. You can look at your Bible while people are occupied in telling the story to each other—and they never notice what you are doing as they are busy telling and listening to the story with each other!

Option 2. Use this option after you have used option 1. People will be braver about volunteering after having already done an STS story together.

Ask if someone will volunteer to retell the story to the entire group. If the listeners act shy and do not respond quickly to your request, say, "Just tell as much as you remember." Smile and keep encouraging the group. Step back and to the side, gesturing for a volunteer to come take your place.

If a story is long or if for whatever reason no one responds (even after multiple invitations AND you have given pauses to allow them to summon courage to step forward) there is a way to embolden a volunteer to retell a story. Say, "I have an idea. Can several of you retell the story? One of you can start it, then another can continue telling it, and another can help until it is all told. And you only need to tell whatever you remember."

Allowing several people to retell the story like that will produce bravery.

(In telling stories in over 25 countries, a volunteer has always come. If it ever happens that no one will volunteer, I plan to take the "blame," and say, "You know, I think I might need to go through this story again so we can be more comfortable with it." Then I would do a Lead Through.)

When you do get a volunteer, applaud or happily acknowledge the person who finally offers to try. Again, smile and say to the volunteer, "You only need to tell the story, not the introduction. Don't worry if you forget some of the story; you have only heard it once. Just start with the part that says…," and then you repeat the first line of the story.

Stand to the side, maybe 10 feet away from the volunteer. If you stand right next to the volunteer, the person will not look at the group and will keep looking at you for approval. If you are too far away, the volunteer feels alone, abandoned. Even as you are standing off to the side while the volunteer retells, make certain that your facial expression and your body language show interest and approval.

Keep your focus on the volunteer. Do NOT use this section of time to talk to anyone else. That person showed trust in you. Earn that trust by truly listening and being attentive.

Afterward, if a story was well told, by your words and expression let the volunteer know how impressed you are with the retelling. Verify that you were listening intently to the volunteer by complimenting something specific the person did, perhaps a gesture or words spoken expressively.

Occasionally, a reteller will not remember much of the story or will tell it very poorly. When this happens, don't ask the other listeners to make corrections. If the group, or even you, correct the volunteer's retelling in front of others, that could embarrass the volunteer.

As well, trying to repair a story that was told with many errors can be very confusing to those learning the story. It is best just to encourage volunteers who have not retold the story well by referencing something they did do well. Maybe say such things as: "I appreciate your bravery," "The part you told about the man being a leper was well told," "I loved the way you dramatized the quotes," or some other specific, encouraging remark.

If your volunteer added information, or embellished the story, that addition needs to be mentioned. Listeners will notice the additions and will wait to see how you address them. If you think it is the loving action to overlook embellishments, so you do not mention (in a kind way of course) that additions are not "approved," you will soon regret that avoidance.

Results of Avoidance. Expect Bible purists to be disappointed that STS allows people to add to the Word of God (and we don't!) Also, others will assume, that they can add what they want when they tell a story.

Actually, you can address these additions kindly. Just give a friendly smile and enthusiastically say, "You are so eager! You even shared extra information with us that I think might not be in the story! This is a challenging task for all of us to say only what is in this one Bible story!"

Most importantly, no matter how good or how poorly the reteller does, remember to find something specific to compliment.

This time of having a volunteer retelling the story is not the place in STS storytelling that people learn the story well enough to be able to tell it perfectly. We do not recommend consecutive retellings of the story by volunteers as a method to learn a story. Since the participants have only heard the story once, the first volunteer will make mistakes. Then when more volunteers tell the story, more mistakes will be made, and the mistakes will become what the people will remember!

If you try to resolve the weakness of that method of consecutive volunteer retellings by publicly correcting the mistakes made by volunteers, the goal of building people's confidence is lost. Only the bravest people will try, and the rest will shrink back and not respond aloud for fear of being publicly shamed.

Although the storyteller could repeat the story correctly, we do not recommend teaching Bible stories to others by having the storyteller tell the same story again and again. Although that can work, it may not be the most exciting way to learn a story! Rote learning by repetition is not fun and can become boring.

Our objective here in the STS process is not to fully teach people the story. Rather, at this point, we want people to learn the story well enough to be able to understand it, discuss it, and make personal application of what they have discovered in the story.

After we go through all the steps of the STS presentation and the story has been fully discussed, there is an ideal time we can make certain the story is precisely known. We call this "creative reinforcement." More details on that come later in this chapter.

The STS process naturally solves most of the challenge of learning a story in the next two steps in the presentation. The Lead Through retelling that comes next often seals the story in people's minds. And beyond that, when storytellers ask the observation questions about the story, they anchor their questions by mentioning each part of the story they want to examine. This way listeners hear the story, part by part, in chronological order, which again reinforces the story's content.

Often, when we to go to a new location somewhere in the world to lead a workshop, local leaders take us aside. They tell us in private, "We don't want you to be disappointed, because these people will not answer questions." When this happens, we thank the leader and respond, "Thank you. We'll just see what happens."

In every case, in every place (much to the local leader's surprise) people ended up answering questions and participating in meaningful discussions. Their willingness to respond grows out of the slow conditioning and encouragement central to the STS process.

Some people take longer than others to develop enough courage to answer questions aloud. They may have been taught not to speak aloud in a Christian teaching environment, while others may just be afraid to make a mistake in public. Many do not believe that they have valid spiritual thoughts to contribute. Actually, we see that, from a variety of past experiences, most people have been conditioned not to think deeply or to consider and discuss new ideas. We love to see that conditioning undone!

Examples of Conditioning Undone
At the end of his first day of exposure to STS, an educated man in his 70s said, "I needed this 40 years ago. We Chinese just don't discuss. We are told what to do and what to believe. This is great. For the first time we can discover for ourselves."

Uneducated villagers in Nepal took awhile to answer questions aloud in a workshop. But they began to warm up as their responses were approved. Eventually everyone became involved in lively discussion. One of the nonliterates there shared, "I didn't know God spoke to people who cannot read."

A Thai instructor reported after a workshop in a village in Thailand, "At first the women would not answer at all. It took several days for them to discover they were allowed to speak, and to discover that what they had to say had value. After that, we couldn't stop them from answering everything!"

Third Time – Lead Through the Story

You first told the story. Then a volunteer retold the story. Now, for your third telling of the story, you ask everyone to go through the story with you.

This is a style of telling the story using frequent hesitations. It is done as if you, the storyteller, need help remembering or recalling a particular detail of the story. You don't want this to feel like a strict test of the listeners' ability to remember the story. Instead, you as the storyteller look expectantly at the listeners, as if you are hoping that someone will say the next few words or sentences. Remember. This is the second time listeners hear the story correctly. Since it is not a general review of some parts, it is essential that you help everyone retell the story—precisely accurately.

Start the story as if you are telling it, except at every phrase or sentence (or maybe at a new thought), you start—then hesitate. Invite the listeners to fill in the rest of the information.

For instance, you could say, "Jesus and His disciples went to a certain city and met there a lady named um…" Then you hesitate and gesture as if you need help and look expectantly, waiting for the people to fill in the blank. After they say "Martha," you respond "Right" or "Good," and then continue leading through the story.

Generally people have the most difficulty recalling names or quantities. To make lead throughs easy, usually we do not ask people to recall a name.

Deciding when to ask for recall of a name takes wisdom. In the short story Martha, Mary and Jesus are mentioned again and again, so listeners can easily recall their names. Use wisdom. Ask easy questions which will help listeners become brave. Then, they will begin to respond more freely to your questions.

Ask, "So who did Martha invite to do what?" After they say, "Martha invited Jesus to come to her home," you say "Good."

Sometimes the storyteller will stop in the story and ask the listeners to tell the next part of the story by saying something such as, "Now Martha had a relative mentioned in the story. Who is it and what are we told about her?" When they answer, "Mary is Martha's sister and Mary sits at Jesus' feet and listens to Him teach," say, "You are correct."

Say, "So Martha has a problem—or something she feels is a problem. What is it?"

To enlist help from the listeners in leading though the story you can hesitate and act as if you do not remember the next part of the story. Use these fill-in-the-gaps or tell-the-next-part methods to encourage the group to recall the story for you.

If here, or at any time, listeners do not respond after you hesitate to allow them to fill in some of the story, start slowly speaking the answer, giving the people opportunity to remember the story and fill in the rest of the sentence or thought.

By providing key words in your questions, you can remind people of the next part of the story. It is vital that your questions contain those key words, because those words act as clues that will prompt the listeners to give an answer from the next part of the story without skipping any information.

Without Key Words. For example, as you review the story, if you say, "And Martha said what?" A listener might correctly respond, "Martha said, 'Tell Mary to come help me.'" Now it is true that Martha did say, "Tell Mary to come help me," so the listener did give a correct answer. But before Martha said, "Tell Mary to come help me," Martha had asked, "Lord, don't you care that Mary has left me alone to do all of the work?" So, by being too general in your review question, you allowed the listener to jump too far ahead in the story.

With Key Words. To help listeners give the answer you want, you can ask a question that reminds listeners of the content of the story. An example would be, "Martha asked Jesus what?" By using the word "ask" in your question, you have wisely guided listeners to recall what Martha asked Jesus.

To help your listeners find more answers, which in turn encourages them to speak up more freely, try to respond in a positive manner, even if the person's answer is not exactly correct.

For example, try this question. "Now what did Martha call Jesus; what title did she use?" They might say "Rabbi" or maybe "Lord." If they answer "Lord," you say that is correct. If they say "Rabbi," you can say, "Right, Martha called Jesus Lord." Even though the listener's answer of "Rabbi" was not exactly correct, the person had the right idea. You are encouraging response, but at the same time gently giving the correct answer to keep the story accurate.

As you lead through the story from the beginning to the end, you can ask such things as: *Who invited Jesus into the home? What is Mary doing in the story? What is Martha busy doing? Then a problem develops. Describe the problem. When Martha speaks to Jesus, what does she call Him? Then what does Martha ask Jesus? How does Martha want to solve the problem? What does Jesus tell Martha that she does too much? So Jesus says, "Mary leave this room immediately!" right? No! You are correct, Jesus did not say that. So what does Jesus say about Mary and her choices?*

Notice that we just suggested saying something that was **obviously** wrong. If you say something wrong in an innocent way, as if you made a mistake, people will want to help you and they will correct the story. This style of helping people to remember the story by saying something wrong will surprise listeners and keep them engaged. But use it sparingly, maybe only once in any lead through.

During this third telling, the story is being locked into the listeners' minds. Additionally, the very easy questions (which are just a review of the story's content) encourage listeners to answer the storyteller's questions out loud. As stated, when people answer these easy questions and are affirmed, they gain confidence. This confidence is needed for the next two parts of STS which are a bit more challenging. Throughout the discussion, listeners are required to look for treasures in the story and report their findings out loud.

Are you ready? Let's try our skills at presentation.

Presentation Phase Two: Discussion of Spiritual Observations

Spiritual Observations. You found a lot of treasures when we looked for the Spiritual Observations and Spiritual Applications. A portion, or all, of these findings could be presented as you teach this story. No doubt more treasures will be found as the Holy Spirit continues to reveal to us all the depth and riches of God's Word.

The following sample questions will lead to some of the many treasures you found, as well as ones that have been discovered in the Martha-Mary story done in workshops all over the world. Notice next that we travel through the story in chronological order, discussing each observation as it fits into the flow of the story.

[The words in italics in each of these numbered observations are the words the storyteller might ask the group. The words not in italics are possible answers or treasures that the group may discover and speak aloud, or words that may be spoken by the storyteller affirming the group's insights.]

1. *In this story, Jesus seems to be complimenting Mary's behavior, but criticizing Martha's. Am I right?* [Wait for answer.] *Now I am confused! Is hospitality a good thing?* [Wait for answer.] *Is preparing a home-cooked meal for guests a nice thing to do?* [Wait for answer.] *So then, what makes me curious is this. Jesus is happy with Mary and not complimenting Martha.*

2. *Besides, if we decide that this story shows us that it is better to do Bible study than to cook a meal, who then will be cooking your meals, gentlemen?* [Wait for answer.] *Also gentlemen, is it a good idea to tell your wives to go into the kitchen to prepare meals for guests when it causes them to miss biblical study, and then tell them that this story teaches that they are doing the less valuable thing?* [Wait for answer.]

   We know that Jesus always speaks truth, but what exactly is that truth that He is speaking? Maybe we should look at this story again?

3. *Remember how we saw that Martha invited Jesus to her home? I wonder, is there anything in the story that could show us if Martha knew that Jesus was someone very special?* [Wait for answer.]

   Listeners may mention that Martha did invite Jesus to her home, that Martha called Jesus "Lord," that Mary was listening to Jesus teach or that when Martha met Jesus He had disciples with Him, so that set Him above the ordinary. All these are valid responses.

4. *We do see in the story that Martha's sister Mary sat at Jesus' feet and listened to Him teach. What does the description of "sitting at his feet" mean to you?* [Wait for answer.] Agreed! Sitting at someone's feet is a way of describing a devoted student/teacher relationship. And as you said, it also shows commitment and identification.

5. *What was it that Martha called Jesus?* [Wait for answer.] *What does "Lord" mean?* [I like to raise my hand to indicate high rank, so people don't think Lord means Martha knew Jesus was God. Wait for answer.] *What might that show us that Martha knew about Jesus?* [Wait for answer.] So she knows Jesus is special, someone she should look up to as superior. She says, "He is Lord," but stays in the kitchen working and does not listen to Him. *What do you think of Martha's behavior?* [Wait for answer.] *Do you see her words and her behavior matching or not matching? How do you see that in this part of the story?*

6. *The story says Martha was overburdened with work and is serving alone. Can we tell from the story what size of a meal or how elaborate of a meal Martha is preparing?* [Wait for answer.] *Can we know if she is preparing simple food, like offering her guests fruit or tea and cookies, or is she serving something more?* [Wait for answer.] *Whose idea was it to invite Jesus to the home?* [Wait for answer.]

    I have a question. If Martha thought Jesus had something valuable to teach, is it surprising that SHE made the choice to do something so time-consuming? What do you think of her decision? [Wait for answer.] *We see Martha complain to Jesus that SHE has too much work to do, but she is the one who chose to use all of her time to cook! What do you think of her reasoning?* [Wait for answer.]

7. *Hmm? What EXACTLY does Martha ask Jesus?* [Wait for answer.] *She says what to whom?* ("Don't you care?") *I wonder. Can Martha's words show us anything about her trust in Jesus?* [Wait for answer.]

8. *What do you think of Martha's solution to her problem? "Jesus, you tell Mary to help me!"* [Wait for answer.] *How is Martha now treating Jesus? Like He is Lord?* [Wait for answer.] I agree. She acts like she is the boss of Jesus and He is her servant! *Does it look like Martha is revealing something about the way she thinks of others? In what way?* [Wait for answer.]

9. *As we listen to the words Martha speaks, and then notice what Jesus says back to her, do you see any reason why Jesus was scolding Martha and complimenting Mary? Jesus says only one thing is what?* [Wait for answer.]

10. *So, what two individuals does Martha blame for her having too much work?* [Wait for answer.] Yes. Mary and Jesus! *How do you see Martha blaming them?* [Wait for answer.] *Martha had asked, "Jesus, don't you care that my sister has left me with all of the work?" Also, note that Martha pointed out that Mary left her with all of the work. But remember, who gave the invitation?* [Wait for answer.] *Who chose to do the big meal?* [Wait for answer.]

    In this story, whose name is not mentioned as being responsible for Martha's overwhelming situation? [Wait for answer.] Yes. Martha does not list herself as having any part in the overwhelming situation.

11. *Notice that Martha made decisions that drew her away from learning from Jesus. But, could Martha's solution to the problem (that she created) have affected anyone else?* [Wait for answer.] Yes. Mary would have had to leave Jesus' presence. *What do you think of Martha's solution?* [Wait for answer.]

12. *What kind of respect does Martha show to Jesus?* [Wait for answer.] The way Martha talks to Jesus shows disrespect. She first accuses Jesus of not caring about her problem, and then she speaks to Him as if He is her servant!

13. *Does Jesus show any kind of emotion in His response to Martha?* [Wait for answer.] Interesting. *How else could Jesus have responded to Martha's accusations and her commanding Jesus what to do—in front of everyone?* [Wait for answer.] I see that too. He could have been really angry at that kind of disrespect, or He could have been so shamed that He left the room. But that is not how he responded. *Describe His way of speaking to Martha.* [Wait for answer.] He kindly explains to Martha that Mary's choice is the better one.

14. *Do you think Martha might be showing disrespect to Jesus in any other ways?* [Wait for answer.] Jesus was a respected teacher. Notice that Martha not only criticized Jesus, she criticized Him in front of His followers! By doing that, Martha again showed no respect at all to Jesus! *Do you see Jesus demonstrating pride or humility in the way that He responded to Martha? How?* [Wait for answer.]

15. *By what Jesus calls Martha, and how He referred to her worry, can we tell whether or not He knew her?* [Wait for answer.] Yes. Jesus shows genuine interest in Martha by using her name when He spoke to her. Jesus uses her name, not once but twice!

16. *Does the story give information that shows us if the way Martha was worrying was something new for her or if it was a habit she had?* [Wait

for answer.] Jesus mentioned to her that she worried about so many things and was concerned, suggesting that it was her habit.

17. *Is there anything in the story that would show whether or not Martha had a choice to stay in the kitchen and prepare a meal, or to sit at Jesus' feet and be taught?* [Wait for answer.] Yes. I agree. Jesus shows us Martha had a choice when He says, "Mary has chosen that which is good." *By those very words of Jesus, what do you see Jesus saying about what Martha chose?* [Wait for answer.]

18. *Jesus said, "Martha, Martha. You worry about so many things and you are so concerned. Mary has chosen the one thing that is necessary." What is Jesus saying here about Martha's choice to make this big meal as compared to Mary's choice?* [Wait for answer.] Mary chose the one thing that was necessary.

19. *Does it seem that Martha thinks what she chose to do is necessary?* [Wait for answer.] *Does Jesus think what Martha is doing is necessary?* [Wait for answer.] *Is eating necessary?* [Wait for answer.] *Please help me understand this. What might Jesus be saying about what was and was not necessary in this story?*

20. *In a culture strong on hospitality, what might have been expected of Mary?* [Wait for answer.] *Did Mary have hard decisions to make? Did Mary have to choose against anything to make her choice?* [Wait for answer.] Ah yes, her culture and her family's expectations.

21. *We saw what Martha did do when she found herself overwhelmed and unable to complete her task. Think for a moment. Was there anything else Martha could have done when she could not handle her load?* [Wait for answers.] Many alternative choices for Martha will be offered. [Encourage people to think of all possible things Martha might have done when she found that she was unable to complete her task.]

22. *What possible resource was available to Martha?* [Wait for answer.] *Who else might Martha have gone to for help?* [Wait for answer.] Very often when we listen to this story and discuss its meaning, the very last suggestion people make is that Martha could have gone to Jesus and asked *Him*, "Lord, I cannot get all of this food preparation and service done. What shall I do?"

23. *Did Martha not go to Jesus and ask Him for help because she was too shy?* [Wait for answer.] *How would you describe Martha's attitude?* [Wait for answer.] *Compare her attitude in this story to Jesus' attitude.*

24. *Compare Martha's choice to Mary's choice. Are they the same or different?* [Wait for answer.] *Which lady is giving to Jesus and which one is receiving from Jesus?* [Wait for answer.] *Which act does Jesus value the most?* [Wait for answer.] *Could that show us anything?* [Wait for answer.]

We hope the listeners discover that Martha is doing something **for** Jesus while Mary is receiving **from** Him. Jesus says the work Martha is doing is not necessary. This can open a great discussion about works and grace!

How Your Questions Will Show Your Style of Teaching

Before you decide how you will form some questions to help people discover the wonderful observations that you have found, we need to look at some of the styles of asking questions that teachers use.

Through the manner storytellers ask questions, they establish how listeners will perceive them as presenters. By the storytellers' tone of voice, expression, body posture and phrasing of questions, they can show various personas, such as a stern schoolmaster, a benevolent professor or a fellow climber.

The stern schoolmaster style does not fit well with STS. That sternness makes the participants feel that, "There is one correct answer, and if I respond incorrectly, I will be publicly shamed." So people hold back and do not respond very much. Since throughout the STS process, we encourage people to use their God-given ability to reason and to discover deep spiritual information from God's Word, we do NOT want to act like a stern schoolmaster!

The benevolent professor is kindly and smiles. But, the wording of the questions by the professor makes it clear that the correct answer is already known. The participants perceive this storyteller to be saying, "I am standing on top of a mountain of knowledge. Will you be smart enough to climb up to the top to show that you have gained the information that I already possess?"

Learners will take part in the discussion. But if you watch carefully, you will see that the small number who respond are the participants who are quick of mind and accustomed to giving correct answers. Those select few love this style of storyteller. For them it is enjoyable to be part of the elite crowd that knows more than most of the rest of the people.

Unfortunately, those in the elite crowd have not thought about the remaining participants in the group who did not join in the discussion.

Those left out never felt smart. They are unsure of themselves. They do not believe they can make the climb.

The fellow-climber storytellers skillfully help all listeners feel that, together, they are climbing a mountain and, together, they are discovering information.

Just know that taking on the persona of a fellow climber is the most challenging role a storyteller can adopt. But, that role is also the most rewarding choice for everyone. It naturally invites everyone to participate and has the least chance of producing pride in the heart of participants and storytellers alike.

Once during a meal break at a workshop, an attendee verified the value of storytellers being fellow climbers. This lady said, "I really liked your *Martha-Mary* story. It made me think a lot. You know what I liked best about it?" Smiling I responded, "What?"

"It was those times that you didn't know the answers yourself and you let us find them for you."

"Oh!" I explained. "This is good. I was able to model what we are teaching in STS. Actually, I have told that story many times around the world, so when I asked the questions, I pretty much knew the answers. But I wanted to give you all the chance to discover, so I held back."

She nodded. "Oh I know that, but I'm talking about all of the places you did not know the answers and you let us find them. I just liked it that you were not afraid to let us see that you do not know everything."

Hmm?—I thought to myself. I've done my job. There is no need to insist that I had already known the things we had explored and that the group discovered. She and the other attendees had wholeheartedly participated. They sensed the "permission" and freedom to think and explore. We literally had climbed the mountain together.

Please note that whenever I present stories that are very familiar to me, the participants still do continue to discover Spiritual Observations and Spiritual Applications new to me—ones that I had not yet recognized. Those new "finds" rarely come as a direct result of me asking a question. Those treasures are found during the lively discussion and from the Holy Spirit's kind way of giving insight to those who listen to Him. The STS forum not only sparks individuals to discover, it also provides a place for people to share with one another what they have just understood.

How to Become a Fellow Climber

The way questions are worded will either encourage or discourage participation. For instance, if a storyteller asks, "Now how many camels did Abraham bring?" The listeners know there's a precise answer. They will think to themselves, *I must say the correct answer.* That type of question creates a classroom feeling and closes down most of the discussion.

Instead, you could use a tone of voice as if you are wondering, and you ask, "So, how many camels was it that Abraham had?…" Your posture, facial expression and tone imply that you're trying to recall the number yourself. That encourages people to volunteer to help. If somebody says, "12," then you could respond, "Let's see now…was it 12 or was it a little more?…" When somebody else says, "It was 14," you can say, "Ahh. I agree. I think it was 14. Thanks. Good answer."

If you act as though you need help, people will more freely respond. Whether it's in the Lead Through or observations or applications, people will feel like they want to help out and will be comfortable enough to join in and give their thoughts, rather than trying to come up with the perfect answers.

You create an atmosphere for people by the style of questions you use. When teachers and pastors lecture, they are usually perceived by those they teach as scholars who know all of the answers. Most people in the world have never experienced discussion as a way to learn. The storyteller can nurture participation for those new at responding to critical-thinking-type questions by showing less of that persona of a schoolmaster who is expecting the "right" answer.

Even as information is uncovered, the storyteller can respond with wonder and delight. You can say things such as: "Oh, I like that." "I think you have something there." Or "That sounds really good."

At times people will share thoughts that do not seem correct or do not fit with the story. As a fellow climber, the storyteller can gently redirect the comment and make corrections by asking for clarification. This redirection will not embarrass the contributor.

For instance, somebody might make a statement and think it's valid, but you are fairly sure it is not in the story. You can say, 'Uhh, help me out, where is that in the story?' Even though you know the statement is not justified in the story, your gentle response allows the person to save face and not be overtly corrected in public. That person will keep that feeling of freedom and be encouraged to continue exploring.

If an idea is shared that you think is incorrect or may be questionable, another gentle way of addressing this is to ask the group for their input. You could say something like, "Hmm, interesting. I wonder what the rest of you think about that? How do we see this in the story?" Again, by allowing the discussion to be with the whole group, you do not elevate yourself to the position of schoolmaster or professor. The Holy Spirit is allowed to be the Master Teacher, and the Word of God becomes the final authority.

Remember, the more you act as though you don't know something, the more helpful people will become. That's the persona that you try to display in asking questions and leading discussions. If you act as if you know everything, people are going to be much more hesitant in answering you. As we said, try not to create a classroom effect because in that environment people are afraid to give a wrong answer.

Preface your questions with conditional words and phrases such as: "I wonder if...?" "Could it be...?" "Does this seem like a possibility...?" "Does this look like...?" "What do you see...?" "What might this mean...?" All of those tentative, searching kinds of phrases help storytellers provide the fellow-discoverer atmosphere.

Probably the most challenging skill of the *Simply The Story* process, that takes the most practice to learn, is the how-to-ask-questions skill. You're not trying to look ignorant or say you don't know something that you actually do know. Rather, it's a way of asking questions that suggests you are a fellow learner. This style of phrasing questions will encourage people to share their answers.

Presentation Phase Two: Discussion of Spiritual Applications

Spiritual Applications. Earlier, when we looked at the *Martha-Mary* story we found some amazing Spiritual Applications. We discovered some important things from God's Word and we also thought about how God might want us to apply those discoveries to our lives today.

The next part of the STS process is to ask questions that lead listeners to discuss and to discover the Spiritual Applications that you have found. This skill both challenges us and provides rewards. You will have to resist the temptation to just hand your listeners the treasures you have discovered. Instead, you need to develop the skill of designing questions that help listeners to discover for themselves the treasures in the story.

What follows are a few sample questions, any of which could be used to help people find some of the applications in the *Martha-Mary* story. As before, when we discovered Spiritual Applications, the story is examined from beginning to end. Notice that each time, before questions are asked, a small part of the story is first restated. Then a few questions are asked that move the listeners' applications from very general and far removed, to more specific and personal applications.

1. *In the story, Mary leaves the kitchen and chooses to spend her time at Jesus' feet learning from Him. Does this have any application to us? Today, can anyone actually sit at Jesus' feet and learn?* [Wait for answer.]

    We hope that listeners will come to the following application. Today, studying God's Word or worshiping God is like listening to Jesus. This could show us that the act of sitting at Jesus' feet shows a sincere interest in the Word of God.

2. *We saw that Martha took on so much work that she was overburdened. Can we today have that problem? What do you think?* [Wait for answer.] *Can we ever say "yes" to too many responsibilities?*

3. *Today, do people in ministry, or even at work or home, ever take on more than they can handle? In what ways can this happen?* [Wait for answer.] *How might we react when some of the ministry work or other work we decide to do begins to overburden us and to take us away from our time of learning from the Lord?* [Wait for answer.]

4. *Do people have choices in life?* [Wait for answer.] *Can people make choices that look good because they are choices to do good work, even Christian work? How might people choose to do something for God when it is nothing He is asking or desiring them to do? Have you ever done that yourself or seen that happen? Can you tell about it?*

    In what ways can our choices to do something for God lead us away from spending time with God? [Wait for answers.] *What should we do when we realize that we find that the ministry work we have decided to do is crowding out the time we need to be spending learning from God?* [Wait for answer.]

5. *Martha blames Mary for not helping serve the guests. Today, when people take on more than they can handle, who or what do people tend to blame? I mean, are people quick to assume responsibility for the overload, or do they blame others for it? What have you observed?* [Wait for answer.]

6. *We saw Martha boldly accuse Jesus of not caring about her problem. Today, do people ever blame others for circumstances or even for decisions they themselves have made?* [Wait for answer.] *Have you*

or people you know ever gone so far as to blame God for decisions they made and then they suggest that God doesn't care? [Wait for answer.]

7. We saw in the story that Martha knew Jesus was a teacher and had followers. She called Jesus "Lord," which is a term meaning that she looked to Him as her leader, her superior. Then she told Jesus what to do to solve her problem. Do people today ever have problems (even ones they create for themselves) and then pray to the God of the Universe and tell Him how to solve them? [Wait for answer.]

   How might people do that? [Wait for answer.] Does it make sense to call God our "Lord," and then tell Him how to solve the problems that we ourselves have caused? What do you think? [Wait for answer.]

8. That's interesting—about accusations. How might God feel when people take on more than they can handle and then they say to God, "Don't you care that others aren't helping me?" [Wait for answer.]

9. We saw that Mary had chosen the good part and yet Martha, her sister, criticized Mary for her decision. Today, does it ever happen that people make good decisions and then they are disrespected and told by someone to do something else? [Wait for answer.] In what ways or places might that happen? Maybe at home, work, school, ministry or even among those to whom we minister? [Wait for answer.]

   What must it feel like to make a good decision and be treated shamefully? [Wait for answer.] We saw how Jesus handled that disrespect. What might we learn from how He responded?

10. Do you think it is possible to be doing physical work, like Martha, and at the same time be learning from God and worshiping? Try to describe what this would be like. [Wait for answer.]

11. On the other hand, do you think someone could be in a location where that person looks like a Mary, learning and studying the Bible, and yet that person's thoughts are actually focused on some work project? [Wait for answer.] Is that something that you (or someone you know) have ever found yourself doing? [Wait for answer.]

12. I was thinking of times when I was reading my Bible or praying and my mind started wandering, and I started thinking about other things, maybe some work I needed to do. Does that ever happen to anyone else? [Pause.] In light of this story of Martha and Mary, how would you describe this mental wandering? [Wait for answer.]

13. *Jesus told Martha that what Mary chose would not be taken away. Today are there decisions people make in regard to their relationship with Jesus such as—placing their faith in Him, seeking a deeper faith commitment or maybe choosing to go into full time ministry—that their families or culture might criticize?* [Wait for answer.] *What kinds of decisions might cause this conflict?* [Wait for answer.]

    Would what Jesus said about Mary's decision, about what He would or would not do as far as interfering with her choice, be meaningful to us today? If so, in what way? [Wait for answer.]

14. *Think about any religion that comes into your mind.* [Pause to let people think.] *In that religion, are its followers doing works for the deity or deities, to appease or impress, or is that religion one of freely receiving from that deity? Compare a religion that places its first importance on good works with what Jesus valued.* [Wait for answer.]

15. *As we saw, when Martha realized that she had more work to do than she could handle, she blamed Mary and Jesus but not herself. When Martha realized her inability to complete the task she thought she needed to do, we saw that she overlooked the resource of asking Jesus what she should do. With this in mind, think again about how we handle our times of over-commitment. What might this story teach us about wise choices?* [Wait for answer.]

16. *Jesus honored Mary when she chose to listen to Him, even when it caused her to go against her culture and the expectations of those around her. What might this teach us?* [Wait for answer.] *In pursuit of knowing God, or spending time with Him, could we ever need to choose against our culture or people's expectations for us? How?*

You just completed the presentation of the Martha-Mary Bible story using *Simply The Story*. You may end your time of ministering in different ways. You can close in prayer, use creative reinforcement (as below), or ask some general questions such as:

- What did you learn in this story?

- What did God show you in this story?

- What did you learn about God?

- What did you discover that might help you this next week?

Another in-depth story exercise on how to prepare questions is in Appendix B: Journey Through a Sample Story.

Creative Reinforcement

A byproduct of this thorough investigation of the story is that people will have learned the story fairly well. After completely investigating a story and making application, storytellers may decide to look for creative ways to help reinforce the story in people's memory.

For instance, in a five-day workshop, attendees are exposed deeply to 21 Bible stories. Afterwards, people need reinforcement to remember the many stories they learned. They need to review them, and they need to practice them to keep them in their memory.

Maybe ask people to practice the story by retelling it to one another? You could ask people to make a song or poem that accurately tells the story. Anything you envision that is oral-style and helps people remember the story accurately is good.

This creative reinforcement is especially beneficial for people who cannot read or do not have a Bible in their language and recorded stories are not available in a language they understand. Participants who are not literate and who belong to a language group that does not have a recorded Bible or Bible stories, need as much help as possible.

It is interesting. Solutions are always obvious—after you find them! Looking into this dilemma allowed us to discover a highly productive solution. If the people who need recorded Bible stories are telling stories in their mother tongue during a workshop—that gives a perfect opportunity to set aside some time in the workshop to record those stories for the people!

A few years into STS, we coined the phrase "Heart Pocket." We said, "Once you have learned a story, the story is in your Heart Pocket."

Later, we found a problem among the nonliterates who were learning hundreds of stories. They knew the stories, but because they couldn't write a list of their stories—they couldn't remember which stories they knew!

That prompted development of our Heart Pocket Books. Calling-card size pages each have a basic picture that instantly brings to mind a specific story. These are not icons to be memorized; they are line drawings that show something unique to just that story. The "pages" are laminated and inserted on a large key ring and become the storyteller's personal Heart Pocket Book. (Literates who learn a lot of stories love these too!)

We thank the Lord for showing His grace by giving us productive solutions.

Chapter 6: General Tips for Leading Discussions

As the discussion moves forward, God can use your past experiences and Bible knowledge to design questions as you teach. The Holy Spirit knows what needs to be discussed and will lead you as you teach.

Probably one of most important skills we can hand off to you, one that will lead to successful discussion of stories is the concept of **Listening and Responding**. You need to listen well to the Word of God as you prepare a story, and as the one who will tell the story, you need to respond to the applications God shows you in the story. Likewise, during the discussion, you listen and respond—listen well to what people say and respond to them.

The Beloved Elder

At a certain time of the day, people in a particular village began to gather around different elders to talk. Some chose to sit with the elder who tells them much wise information. Others wanted to be with the elder who is known to sit and listen to all that the people have to say. But most of those in the village wanted to spend time with one special elder. In fact, this village affectionately called him the "Beloved Elder."

Although the Beloved Elder does speak much wise information, he also listens well. But, beyond those skills, this beloved one shows added insight. He knows how to pass on his wisdom by giving people an opportunity to think and to discover. Even though he possesses greater knowledge than his people, he encourages those who come to him to share and offer their ideas. Often this elder does not speak—even though he knows answers to questions. This allows those who come to him to learn to think and to solve problems.

This beloved elder encourages his sons—and even his wife and daughters, to voice their thoughts. He has no fear of allowing others to speak, because he knows that he possesses great knowledge. He knows that the more he can give courage and confidence to those he leads, the more they will treasure his leadership.

As well, his followers copy his leadership style and, in turn, they encourage others to discover wisdom. This elder's children have grown up to be wise and confident, and they walk in their father's path.

The Bible tells of a time early in Jesus' ministry on earth when more than 5,000 people came to hear Him teach. But these people needed food.

Jesus first asked a question and gave Philip and His disciples a chance to think of how they might solve the problem. But none showed the maturity to ask Jesus to do a miracle. So Jesus showed them the answer by performing a miracle and turning one boy's supply into food for everyone.

Again and again, Jesus gave His disciples, and others, an opportunity to think and to answer questions using a godly perspective. For three years Jesus continued to train His disciples by encouraging them to listen to His words and to think and believe, and to apply wisdom. Jesus was preparing them to serve and lead others.

Today, when Bible passages are discussed STS style, many involved in the discussions are leaders in their families and in ministries, so they have more knowledge than those they teach and guide. We applaud leaders who are not the first every time to tell their answers to questions.

What a joy it is to watch these wise, confident leaders allowing others to respond. These leaders see the value of encouraging people to think and to be responsible for their thoughts. Like the Beloved Elder, and like Jesus, these leaders know how to inspire confidence in others. These leaders also know when their deep wisdom is needed, and they freely share information at the right times.

The Challenges of Listening and Responding

As you are first trying to acquire the skills involved in STS, there is much to remember. Those new to STS focus intently on their STS presentation, telling the story, the order of the process and asking questions. Interestingly, these new presenters tend to concentrate so much on the process that something vital is often left out—The People! Your task is to discuss a Bible story with others. By not listening well to what people say and ask, by not responding to their contributions, there is no discussion.

One of the best mental doorways to enter that encourages thinking is the doorway of conversation. After you have spent time discovering many valuable treasures in a story, it should be pleasurable to talk about the story with other people. So instead of thinking about YOUR "presentation" and everything YOU plan to say, ask questions and listen to what people say. Talk to them ABOUT the story. Have a conversation with them.

During the conversation, you will use some of your prepared questions to prompt conversation as you move through the story. Hopefully, your questions will help people discover some treasures you found during your time of preparation. Most of us talk with others every day and we do this—without a written script! We converse about things that interest us. Relax and engage in a conversation about the Bible story!

Actually, Listening and Responding is so central to the process, that we say, "The definition of STS is Listening and Responding."

Listening and Responding in Action

One of the many stories we explore in STS is the 23rd Psalm. Most who know the Bible, even a little, are familiar with that passage. But going through it slowly, and asking questions that help us to deeply hear what God gave us in that Psalm, can be amazing.

Sometime back, Ramesh, our director in the Buddhist world, told me that he had been teaching the 23rd Psalm the STS way. (Now mind you, I taught this man who lives in Nepal how to do STS!) It seemed like a fun idea that he would try to do STS with a Psalm. So I asked, "Will you teach it to me?" That day became a time I hope never to forget.

Look in this report for my slowness to listen to the story and listen to the storyteller. And as well, look at the way Ramesh kept putting out bread-crumb clues to bring me close to a treasure, and made himself hold back and let me discover. He would listen to me and then give a clue to bring me closer to discovery.

He did ask questions about the whole story, but one particular thread of information Ramesh followed still stands out today. I will bypass the many questions he asked that developed the whole story and just include here that one thread.

Ramesh asked, "At first, how does the sheep refer to the shepherd?"

I gave the answer I had learned years before. "MY shepherd. That shows us that we can know the Lord Jesus in a personal way."

But Ramesh would not allow me to jump ahead like that. In STS we first listen carefully to what the story says, and only after that do we make application of the information to ourselves.

Ramesh forced me to slow down and listen to what the story said and to look at this familiar passage more carefully. He kept making me listen to the story.

I agreed to listen, thinking I could check his technique. Frankly, I was wondering what my student would be able to show me in a passage that I knew so well, had taught many times, and even written about in articles.

"This is a sheep talking, is it not?" asked Ramesh.

I nodded in agreement.

"Well, how does the sheep talk about the shepherd? How does the sheep refer to the shepherd?"

I asked, "Do you mean how the sheep calls the shepherd 'he'?"

"That's right," responded Ramesh. "But don't you see where the sheep sees the shepherd?"

"Uh? What?" I was not getting it.

"Where is the sheep in relation to the shepherd? See it?" Ramesh was pressing intently, as he wanted me to see something I was not yet finding. (In STS, we try not to push at people to make them see what we have found in a story. But at this point Ramesh, being the one who I had always taught, wanted desperately to share something with me. In this particular listening and responding scenario, since we knew one another well, Ramesh knew that persistently pressing me to slow down and think about the story was acceptable.)

"Umm, I guess if the sheep is being led, that puts the shepherd in front of the sheep?"

"YES! That's it," Ramesh said. "And now go on in the story to the Valley of the Shadow of Death part. How does the sheep refer to the shepherd?"

"He?" I answered.

"Oh! Look again," prompted Ramesh. "The story says, 'and I will fear no evil for who is with me?' What did the sheep call the shepherd? How did the sheep refer to the shepherd?"

"Wait," I blurted out. "It is 'Thou!' Wow. There is a change! I had never noticed that before. Now the sheep is talking TO the shepherd, not about the shepherd! That is rich."

"Yes. And keep looking. Do you see where the shepherd is? What changed? Look at it!"

"Look at what?" I asked.

"Look at what else changed. Look at it. Before, the shepherd was in front of the sheep. Now where is the shepherd?"

"Okay, now I see it," I burst out. "First the shepherd was in front of the sheep, now he is with the sheep."

"Yes! At first he was in front, and now he is beside," beamed Ramesh. "But that is not all. Keep looking. The story says 'Thou' again. The sheep says, 'Thou anointest my head with oil.' If the shepherd is putting oil on the sheep's head, where do you see the shepherd now?"

"I see that! Over the sheep! The shepherd is over the sheep."

"Keep going," Ramesh encouraged. "The story says, 'Surely goodness and mercy shall follow me all the days of my life.' The sheep is saying where else he feels the shepherd's presence to be. Do you see that?"

"Yes I do. That is amazing."

By now Ramesh was beaming. "The shepherd is in front and beside and over and behind. He is all around the sheep."

From there, since we were at the end of the story, we both went to the applications. How could we not? We both chattered about various applications to us today from what we had seen together in the story. But that whole new thread of discovery, how Jesus our Shepherd is in front, beside, over, and behind us, dominated our conversation. What a comforting realization that was!

Post Script. Sometime later in the office, the staff was talking about the mistakes we were all making as we worked in this ministry, and how again and again God showed us mercy and helped us past them. I commented, "God really has our backs! On a daily basis, as we address our challenges, God is our strong support. He says, 'Go ahead and don't worry. I'll cover you. I will make sure no one sneaks up behind to hurt you.'"

Then that Psalm story came back to me. "Oh my! That's the 23rd Psalm! 'God has our backs covered' is today's way of saying 'surely goodness and mercy shall follow me all the days of my life.'"

Hmm? Teacher listens to student—both hear from a familiar passage.

Interchanges such as these, where indigenous believers are teaching leaders from Europe and the West, are becoming more frequent. Missionaries in multiple countries such as India, Togo, Mozambique, Niger and the Philippines have been coming to indigenous instructors to be trained in STS.

Ultimately, STS is just people—who are listening to people—who are listening to God's Word. Listening and responding is available to all. And the results demonstrate that it is not just top tier leaders who hear from God and then dispense their knowledge to others. In fact, those indigenous instructors who by request are training missionaries are 3rd and 4th generation learners of STS!

Details That Lead To Success

We hope those reports just inspired you to continue learning about STS and acquiring some of its new skills. Let's start with a part that stretches literate learners. Even though you might think it is impossible to remember your questions without writing them down, it is important to NOT write out the questions that you want to ask about the story. To recall your questions, mentally go through the story, letting the story itself remind you of your prepared questions. The story becomes your way to remember; **the story becomes your notes!**

Rethink Your Introduction. Now that you have discovered many treasures hidden inside your story, you may want to add to, or shrink, the introduction that you prepared. If you find that the information in your introduction is actually contained in the story, you would be wise to take those facts out of the introduction.

For instance, you may have originally planned to introduce the Abram story in Genesis 12:1-9 by saying, "This story is about a man who is called by God to leave his people and his country and to start a new nation." However, after you have spent some time thinking about that passage as you were hunting for spiritual treasures, you now realize that particular information about Abram is contained inside the story. So, you can take that information out of your introduction.

If, however, you have found some insight about a story that would be better understood by giving a small amount of added information about it, then tell the information in your introduction.

For instance, one of the many treasures in the *Martha-Mary* story is based on Martha's choice to make an elaborate meal for many guests. Another treasure is the shock that Martha shows such disrespect to Jesus by criticizing and bossing Jesus in the presence of His followers. The story does begin that Jesus and his disciples enter a certain town. But in the story we are only told that Martha invited Jesus to her home. It is not stated in the story that the disciples came with Jesus.

To give clarity to the discussion, it is wise to give the story an introduction something like this. "When Jesus lived on earth He chose men to go with Him. These men, called disciples, always traveled with Jesus, except when we are told that Jesus went away by Himself for a time or in some cases when Jesus took just a few of the disciples apart from the others for a short time." This information helps listeners to realize that the visit by Jesus also included his disciples.

As a storyteller, you should always assume that one or more people present do not have knowledge of the Bible other than what is told them in the story and in the introduction. So to have successful STS discussion, it is always necessary that the information needed to answer your questions has already been provided in your introduction or is in the story.

If you have taught some stories to everyone present, you CAN ask questions that build on any information gained from those earlier story times together. Just keep in your mind that most stories have ample information inside them, so usually you do not have to go to other places in the Bible to teach a story well.

Occasionally, providing added information in the introduction, such as God's rules pertaining to lepers, the Sabbath, eating, or how Jews felt about Samaritans, can give depth to the events in a story.

Also, after you have completed discussing the story, you may want to introduce something within the story that has obvious symbolic or typological significance. You help listeners discover this symbolic meaning by telling them yet another "story." You take them to a new story or a few verses from another passage in the Bible. Tell it STS style. Do this if you believe your listeners have really grasped the deeper spiritual parts within the story you are presenting, or simply if the Holy Spirit leads you to do so!

The added information you give about the story should be obvious enough that the listeners can easily make the application. Begin by saying something like, "There is another story that occurred long after this one." Then you take them to a passage that contains some typology or symbolism. Most often that second story will be one in the New Testament.

For example, if you had told the story of *Moses and the Brass Serpent* in Numbers 21:4-9, and your group had completed discovering and applying the Spiritual Applications, you may feel led to say this:

"It will be a long time before we can discuss all of the stories in the Bible together. There is a story that comes much later in the Bible that I want to tell you next. It might help us to discover even more in this story of *Moses and the Brass Serpent*. [If you have time, you would give a short introduction and then tell John 3:1-16. If the time is limited, you could give a short introduction including main parts of verses 1-13, and then tell the short "story" that Jesus told that religious man in verses 14-16. Remember, tell it STS style!]

> And as Moses lifted up the serpent in the wilderness, even so must the Son of man be lifted up: That whosoever believeth in him should not perish, but have eternal life. For God so loved the world, that he gave his only begotten Son, that whosoever believeth in him should not perish, but have everlasting life.

Listen to the Responses of the Listeners to the Story. The answers people give will help you to sense their needs and their personal questions. Those insights will help you form original questions as you continue. This is called "teaching from the moment."

Most Questions Should Be About What People Did or What God Did. These questions will move listeners toward discovering spiritual truths. Just review the actions and the words each character spoke. Be careful about asking "why" questions as they may invite speculation and guesses that cannot be backed up by Scripture. Using questions that ask "what" are usually the best. Interestingly, the answers to several "what" questions can lead everyone to discover the answer to an unvoiced "why" question!

Ask Observation Questions. After restating a small segment of the first part of a story, maybe say this: "Could anything in this first part of the story show us something about the beliefs of (select characters in the story)?" "How might the story show us what that person valued?"

Say: "Does anything in this section show us something about the character of God?" or "Do we see faithfulness here?" As you explore each part of the story, see if those in the story, by their actions or words, demonstrated disrespect, or fear, or confusion, or greediness, or kindness or bravery, or trust, or wisdom. Make sure that the questions you ask can be answered from the information contained inside the story that you just told.

On any of those questions that invited yes or no responses, you can then follow up the "yes" responses with a question such as, "Help us out. How (where) in this part of the story do you see that?"

Gradually Help Listeners Make Applications of the Truths in the Story. As you move through your discussion in the treasure hunt for Spiritual Applications, listen carefully to people. Listen for opportunities to ask if they, or someone they know, have ever had the same feelings and reactions as they saw in the people in the story (doubt, fear, faith, hope, confusion etc). When you hear a "yes" or see body movements that indicate a "yes," that is a good time to ask, "Would someone like to share that experience?"

Share Personal Applications. When you have completed discussing applications, if you are led by God to do so, you may share how some part of the story touched you. Or, you can ask if some particular part of the story impacted them.

Vital Elements of Good Questions. Answers to your questions must be:

- Contained in the story.
- Provable by the story.

Information Outside the Story. If a very important insight or application in the story requires an outside verse to show that truth, you can include that scriptural information in the introduction to the story. Likewise, the additional Scripture can be given after all applications provable from within the story have been presented.

Do this only on rare occasions, because use of Scripture outside the story makes the listener dependent on the storyteller's research instead of just listening to the story. Storytellers can ask questions built on Bible information that they know listeners have gained during previous times of storytelling.

Good Answers. When people offer acceptable answers, encourage them. Say such things as, "Good answer," "I never thought of that," or "That makes sense."

Not So Good Answers. If you think answers given by listeners are incorrect, you might say, "Let's go back and see if that matches the story." If the conclusions they reached are wrong, you might want to take the blame and say, "Sorry, I did not make that part clear" or "Maybe my question was not worded well."

If an answer or a question from a listener is totally off of the subject, you can say, "That would be a topic we could discuss another time," or "Maybe in the next story we will find the answer." Some questions are trails that lead to nowhere and the whole group will go off of the main path if you take time to answer them.

If Groups are Large or Time Is Short. Asking questions and responding to the listeners' responses is the standard way one uses STS. If the time available does not allow fielding answers or the circumstance or size of the listening group rules out receiving answers, there is an option. Teachers using STS can ask rhetorical questions. Listeners are asked to think of answers to the questions, but not to speak them out loud. As the storyteller, just make sure that you allow a slight moment for the listeners to think of their answers.

Keeping Accuracy: Value of Review

One of the advantages in the discussion style of STS is the powerful tool of "review."

Review in STS is most valuable when Bible stories are presented in chronological order. Instead of the teacher giving an introduction before beginning the story, the teacher can ask those hearing the stories to give a brief review of the previous meeting's story and discoveries.

Because new people might be present during a teaching session, or perhaps some regular attendees did not come to the previous gathering, a review of the last story will help those who missed it. Having learners take responsibility for the review give people an opportunity to repeat the story from memory.

Also, members should be asked to share some of the treasures previously found and what they learned. Review allows people to solidify the information in their minds and to speak Scripture to others. This is a perfect place in the meeting to hear testimonies of attendees about their use of that story during that previous week.

As well, when class members are given opportunity to share what they have learned during the previous meeting together, the teacher is able to make certain that the last story and its treasures were correctly and well understood. If people who were in the prior teaching are vague about what they learned or cannot tell the story, it is a signal to the teacher to do a review for everyone.

There is no reason to move ahead into a new story until the last story is well understood by everyone.

Chapter 7: Accurate Application –
Finding the Elephant

As storytellers increase their investigative skill, they begin to notice details they may have previously missed in the passages they are studying. No matter how small, what a thrill each discovery brings! However, as those small interesting parts are found, storytellers must be careful not to lose sight of the whole. Storytellers must always remember that the Bible is more than a history book. They must not miss the spiritual message or messages that the small parts of the story bring.

For instance, people often tell the story of David and Goliath. They preach or lead a discussion about David being a small, young boy who had developed a great skill and who was brave and confident enough to face a giant and to conquer him. Then an application is made: "You should all be like David and be brave in the face of great odds."

Nice message. But, is that all there is to this story?

Although the story does contain that preached information, the larger spiritual messages of the story were overlooked. According to the story, David knew that his God was able to defeat the giant and the opposing army who were trusting in false gods. In addition, the army of Israel and Saul their King, who should have been relying on God to defeat the giant and the false gods these enemies worshiped, missed their opportunity to trust God in battle. The nation that worshiped false gods was defeated when one seemingly insignificant person walked in faith.

In all stories, as you find many worthwhile, small truths, make sure you listen well to the whole story so that you can grab hold of the overriding spiritual truths that truly are contained in the story.

The finding-the-elephant principle can help remind each of us, as storytellers, to maintain overall accuracy of a story as we hunt for the many spiritual treasures it will contain.

First, a case of **Missing the Elephant:**

You may have heard a tale similar to this before. Five blind men were led to an elephant and were told, "Men, you are standing by an elephant. Please describe it." Immediately, four of the men began feeling whatever part of the elephant that they first touched.

One felt the tail and described the elephant by saying, "It's a small tree branch."

A second blind man handled the elephant's ear, and he said, "An elephant must be a giant leaf on a tree."

One man felt the elephant's trunk and jumped back. "It's a long snake!"

The fourth man tried to reach around the elephant's belly. He couldn't. So he explained, "An elephant is a huge round rock; but it is not as hard as a rock, I know—and it moves!"

The fifth blind man scoffed, "Oh, I don't need to feel the elephant to describe it. I have heard that loud elephant-trumpet sound many times. Everyone knows that an elephant is a big musical instrument!"

Each man tried to describe a part of the elephant, but they missed. None understood the parts, so they missed the whole. They missed the elephant.

When we look for treasures in a Bible story, we must remember that there is a wholeness to every story. We call this wholeness, "The Elephant." When a story is long, there are often several parts to it, similar to a drama that has more than one act. In those long stories, each act or scene may contain its own elephant of truth.

Sometimes, when we read through a familiar story, we might have a preconceived idea of what the story is about, so we fail to really listen to it. Remember the one blind man who didn't even take the time to investigate, because he was so convinced that an elephant was a musical instrument? We, too, can think that we already know all about a Bible passage, and, as a result, we totally miss the overall truth of the story.

As well, it is easy to commit the same mistake the blind men made. We do this by grabbing hold of some individual parts of a story—and then just stop there. By failing to stand back to consider the whole story, and the way all of its parts fit together, we might miss the whole elephant.

It takes careful listening and prayer to make sure that we accurately grasp the complete story. Those individual truths you discover have value, but those individual parts still may not describe the whole elephant well.

Example of Finding the Elephant in a Bible Story

First read Mark 1:40-45. Then take time to look for the elephant:

> And there came a leper to him, beseeching him, and kneeling down to him, and saying unto him, If thou wilt, thou canst make me clean. And Jesus, moved with compassion, put forth his hand, and touched him, and saith unto him, I will; be

thou clean. And as soon as he had spoken, immediately the leprosy departed from him, and he was cleansed.

And he straitly charged him, and forthwith sent him away; And saith unto him, See thou say nothing to any man: but go thy way, shew thyself to the priest, and offer for thy cleansing those things which Moses commanded, for a testimony unto them. But he went out, and began to publish it much, and to blaze abroad the matter, insomuch that Jesus could no more openly enter into the city, but was without in desert places: and they came to him from every quarter.

Of course there are many wonderful and important treasures in this story. But do you see the elephant? Often teachers miss it.

They do see such things as:

1. The man's faith that Jesus could make him clean.
2. Jesus' willingness to make him clean.
3. Jesus' ability to heal.
4. Jesus' compassion and tenderness.
5. Jesus showing his love by even touching a leper.
6. Jesus' identification with an untouchable.

But then, they also make some of these other "interesting" observations:

1. Jesus did tell the man not to tell anyone about the healing, but to go and show himself to the priest. But this man was so full of excitement that he couldn't contain himself, so he shared his healing with everyone and gave testimony as to what Jesus had done. The application is made by preaching on joy and appreciation.
2. Although the healed man was not supposed to tell people what had happened, for joy he could not help but witness. The application is made about the importance of witnessing.
3. Because this man burst forth to tell everyone of his healing, Jesus had to go out of the cities and "they came to him from every quarter." As a result of the man's proclaiming the news, even more people than before were able to come to Jesus for healing. The application is made on how God's sovereign will was accomplished through the healed man.

Let's now take a look at this story and see how many wonderful treasures make up the whole.

Do all of those nine treasures just listed give an accurate overview of the story, or do any miss a deep part of the story? Is it possible that only half of an elephant was discovered?

It is important to discuss the many treasures in the story, such as the healing and the leper's faith to be healed. But, if we overlook something in the story, or teach something not in the story, we might miss its spiritual wholeness.

We listen to this story, hear certain key phrases and then talk about what happened that day. We all love the idea of bold witnessing about Jesus, so we see the man's actions as good. After all—the man told a lot of people in many places about what Jesus had done! As well, we love opportunities to speak about the sovereignty of God, so we feature that.

Let's go slowly through just one part of this story to see what we might discover.

What did Jesus tell the healed leper about things to do and not to do? ...

Were those two instructions spoken as suggested options to the newly cleansed man? ...

No. Actually, Jesus sternly commanded the man NOT to tell anything to anyone about his newly-cleansed condition. He was to go to the priests and fulfill the ordinances to be declared clean and do the sacrifices, all as a testimony to the priests!

So, are we following what the story says when we use it to teach about unrestrained joy, the glories of witnessing, or the sovereignty of God? The Lord did give us enough information in the overall passage to enable us to grasp what happened that day.

If we fail to listen well to the story, we will miss the elephant!

Well-prepared storyteller-teachers look at the context of the story first. The words just before this story show something about Jesus' will.

> And he said unto them, Let us go into the next towns, that I may preach there also: for therefore came I forth. And he preached in their synagogues throughout all Galilee, and cast out devils. (Mark 1:38-39)

Did you notice that Scripture tells us in verse 38 that Jesus wanted to go into the next towns?

What did Jesus want the leper to do in relation to the priests?... In the story, Jesus sternly commanded the cleansed leper to show himself to the priest, and make an offering for his cleansing according to the things that Moses had commanded. So first of all, we see that Jesus' instructions to be obedient to the Mosaic Law were disregarded by the healed leper and, as well, the leper was not legally cleansed according to the law.

Jesus' strong instructions to the leper, that the leper was to show himself as a testimony to the priests, was not obeyed. By the story, can we tell if Jesus wanted the priests to know about and to authenticate the healing?... So who was shown respect by the cleansed man? Jesus? The priests? God's laws in the Old Testament?... Right. Not to anyone but himself!

After the healing, due to that one man's willfulness, God tells us in the story that Jesus could no longer go openly into the town.

The cleansing and the leper's faith to be healed, and the many wonderful things we see about Jesus are great truths. But, if we miss the truth of the leper's disobedience and his disrespect of Jesus, the One who just healed him, we miss the other half of the elephant.

Just as we take seriously the information on healing, so we must take seriously the cleansed leper's disobedience.

This latter part of the story is not about joy or witnessing; it is about self will. It is about those who ask for and receive a life-changing gift from God and then live in disobedience to His commands.

By carefully reading the story (and not inserting our ideas into the story), this whole truth, the elephant, can be found: Jesus miraculously and with compassion brought new life to an untouchable, a man who then followed his own will and disobeyed the One who just healed him. That is the elephant that gets overlooked in this story.

The leper seems to have more focus on the healing than the healer. Throughout the Bible, in many stories, we see people making that same mistake. People commit "religious" sins. In their zeal, they do works "for God" without listening to or respecting what God had told them to do! Is it wrong to testify? No—in fact we are told to be witnesses. Was it wrong in Jesus' plan for that particular time and place? Absolutely!

A classic example of how God views those who do something that appears to be correct, even something religious, is in 1 Samuel. There we see one person performing a religious act, but the timing and the circumstances of the act is wrapped in disobedience to a directive of God. The Lord compares this disregard of His directives to the very worst kinds of sin.

Hath the LORD as great delight in burnt offerings and sacrifices, as in obeying the voice of the LORD? Behold, to obey is better than sacrifice, and to hearken than the fat of rams. For rebellion is as the sin of witchcraft, and stubbornness is as iniquity and idolatry. (1 Samuel 15:22-23)

Condoning, or even justifying, the leper's disobedience when we lead a discussion on this story, gives license to probably what is mankind's most common sin. Sometimes this sin is subtle, because we have not spoken out loud, "I choose my way over God's." But if we ignore what God has said and choose instead to focus on what we want to do, it is sin. Lack of obedience is disobedience.

We cannot overlook this second part of the story, the act and result of the disobedience. If we excuse the leper's disobedience for any reason, we encourage this common sin of deciding to override God's will with our will. How sad it is to hear believers today say, "Oh I know what God says in His Word about this situation, but I have good reasons for doing it differently." Funny, we rarely hear people describe their actions in this way. "I am going to disobey God's Word because I make better decisions than He does."

We selected this passage because many teachers fail to listen to it well. We wanted to illustrate how easily we can miss the wholeness of a story and in so doing miss teaching God's whole message.

It is a solemn responsibility to teach the Word, even a story. This elephant illustration is used to remind us to carefully and thoroughly listen to all of what God says. As the Bible says, "He that hath an ear let him hear."

When teaching using STS concepts, we must listen to the whole story very carefully and pray to understand and trust what God says in the story. We want to see how the individual parts of a story show us the whole story.

In the leper story, God lets us see the consequences of disobedience. However, notice that in many other Bible stories, we are not shown the consequences of people's sin. We can also teach from those stories the wisdom of obeying God because we trust His leadership, not just because we fear the consequences of disobeying.

By teaching this story from Mark in its wholeness, people can learn about the sadness and consequences of disobedience to the Savior who brings us life as well as the joy of healing. If we gloss over, or miss altogether the disobedience in this story, we have failed the story and failed to encourage believers to obey God by faith.

Chapter 8: Nonliterates and
Oral Bible Schools

Workshops With Literates and Nonliterates Together

Often nonreaders attend STS workshops. So the stories that need to be learned by these nonreading attendees must be read to them, told to them, or played for them on some kind of audio player.

When recorded stories are needed in workshops, we use solar-powered audio players, produced by MegaVoice and others, with *God's Story* and a New Testament (if available) in the graduates' mother tongue. As well, The God's Story Project continues to record and add Bible stories to the players.

After workshops, one player is given for each village represented in the workshop. The recipient is the custodian of the player, but shares the player with other attendees. The player enables everyone to learn many more stories.

In most cases, the whole village enjoys listening to the Bible stories. Very often the workshop attendees consider the player so valuable (and it is to these nonliterates) that they hand off their precious gift to their pastor. The pastors use them in ministry. The players serve as a source for all of the nonliterates in the region to learn more Bible stories. Wonderfully, the recordings serve as a reference point to keep the stories accurate.

Interestingly, the same STS training as outlined in this handbook is given around the world—to literates and nonliterates—in the same workshop. Often, these nonreaders show more ability to learn a story, and to tell it well, than those who can read the story to learn it.

Surprisingly to some, nonliterate learners show keen ability to locate multiple spiritual treasures within the story. However, every learner, literate and nonliterate, struggles at first to form questions that lead others to treasures through discussion. Keep in mind that forming questions is an acquired skill that is available to literate and nonliterate alike.

An Unexpected Application.
In a workshop in Dwaniro, Uganda, an old man delivered a message that both the Africa TGSP Director and I hope we will never forget. The Africa director, whose roots are "village," gave me this report.

"The people here are poor and almost none of the believers in this workshop can read. This place is very primitive!

"One particular storyteller I observed stood under a tree and presented his first STS story to a group of five men who had not studied that particular story. This very old man, maybe 65 years old, had just told the story of the *Lost Axe Head* from Second Kings. I watched as he led the men in a discussion about the story.

"Then, as the storyteller moved through the applications, he asked, 'Remember how Elisha's student was so upset, because the axe head he lost was borrowed?' The men in his group nodded knowingly. 'And we talked about how Elisha and God showed interest and helped that student find his borrowed axe-head?'

"'What do you have in your house that is borrowed?' The men looked at one another and then shrugged their shoulders.

"The storyteller persisted. 'What do you have in your house that you do not own?' Again these villagers, who had very little at all in their houses, shook their heads explaining, 'We have nothing in our homes that is not ours.'

"The storyteller became slightly frustrated, because the other men were not seeing a discovery that he himself had found. So he blurted out, 'What about your wives? Do you own them?'

"'Yes. We own them' was the united response. 'We paid four goats for them!'

"'I know,' the storyteller responded. 'But who gave life to those goats, and who gave you the ability to raise those goats?—God! So it is God who owns your wives, not you!' The men exchanged some serious looks and then agreed with the storyteller.

"'Well, how are you treating your wives—as if they are yours and not borrowed from God? I beat my wife and kick her like she is my possession and I can do that when I want to—but she is borrowed, not mine! I must treat her like she belongs to God—and my children too.'

"At that he started to cry and turned away in shame and began to repent to God. And the other men sobered as the Holy Spirit told them the same message. Tears began to roll down their faces too. The presentation stopped while a time of repentance took place."

As this story was being related to me, my mind was whirling. *Is that message really in the story? I know placing value on something borrowed is in the story. But, is this a valid application? Apparently it was valid for those men that day!* And then I thought, *Oh my! How do I treat my staff, as if they are mine to berate when they make a mistake, or do I treat them as on loan from God?* Conviction came to my heart as well.

[Had this nonliterate old man used logic and inductive reasoning to understand and apply the Word of God? Had he used questions to help other village men discover important truth in the story? Can a literate ministry leader, who knows the Word, be taught a spiritual application by a nonliterate from another culture? Yes, Yes and Yes!]

Oral Bible Schools

Oral Bible Schools (OBSs) sprang from interest shown at the workshops in deeper Bible study. Local pastors and leaders asked for more opportunity to learn stories in community, which prompted this design for the schools.

Those interested in joining an OBS submit an application, or pastors of local congregations nominate people to be part of the student body. Twelve people are selected, most of whom have attended a workshop. Then the selected students receive special training for one additional week by an STS instructor. That instructor moves into the role of the OBS overseer.

Most schools have a one-year design. Over the course of that year, students meet for two weeks at a time and then go home for two weeks. Some commute daily. The overseer visits the school for three days at the end of each two-week session. Students purchase their own food locally or bring food with them. Local pastors and believers give housing to the students as needed.

The students' curriculum is learning and using STS to discuss 210 Bible stories from throughout the Bible. If, by the end of the school term, anyone does not know all of the stories, that person waits to graduate until all of the stories are learned. Gaining skill on leading STS workshops and doing outreaches, they call "practicals," are also part of the training.

One bishop arranged a unique OBS. People from his churches who work in the flower fields meet daily at lunch. He set these up in four different locations where they learn and discuss five stories a week. Other workers wanted to hear the stories, so they joined in to listen. Within the first four months, so many people were saved that 16 new churches were planted.

Some other "business" OBSs meet every day after work. Both of these school models have 210 stories as their goal.

In India, some OBSs are held in homes every evening. Three or four families make up a school.

One innovative leader in the Philippines does a weekly radio program. He tells a Bible story STS style to a small live audience in studio. People phone in or send text responses to his questions. Some of the messages have come from regions occupied by terrorists!

He then decided to lead a workshop on the radio. The success of the radio-workshop was verified when this leader-storyteller began talking on air about the OBSs. Callers who had gone through the radio-workshop phoned in and asked, "Why can't we have a school on our island?"

From that request, "mobile" OBSs started. In three locations, groups of 7, 13 and 17 met together in their own locations and learned stories. Three times weekly the school students phone the STS instructors to tell their stories and to talk about their findings in the stories.

Within the first two years of establishing those various formats, the number of STS Oral Bible Schools in session—in a total of nine countries—went from one to sixty!

Approximately 40% of the OBS students are educated and have diplomas from Bible schools. Most of them already serve as pastors or evangelists.

The completion rate for students in the OBSs is—95%!

Impact of an Oral Bible School – Shock, Surprise, Then Awe

Imagine the shock when our Africa director phoned with this urgent question. "The staff that started the workshop on Lake Victoria Island just encountered a new problem. The people in this region are polygamists. But not just that, the host and most of the pastors and leaders in the workshop are polygamists too! What should we do? Should we select some specific stories to address this problem?"

After that initial shock, I sought the Lord about what stories to use. Very quickly He reminded me of what we continually say. "You do not have to pick out specific stories to teach people the lessons you want them to learn. The Holy Spirit will use the regular workshop stories to deliver the messages He has for each person hearing the story."

"Are you sure?" our director asked. "Remember how remote this place is? The instructor who phoned me is waiting on a tree limb. There is only one place at the end of that island where they can get cell reception—and they have to climb a tree to get it! Is this your final answer?"

I assured him that it was the answer that I thought the Lord would want. Although it was obvious to us that polygamy should not be part of these people's Christian lives, I wanted the Lord to address it in His time. So the instructor climbed down the tree, and we all prayed!

After the workshop, the team returned home and sent this report to us:

"On the third day of the training, one of the groups preparing a story got into a strong discussion about—you guessed it—polygamy! Amazingly, no instructor had brought up the topic! Nothing was resolved, but the Holy Spirit planted a seed in their hearts.

"These believers and their pastors surrounded us and said, 'This is the first visit to our island by any Christian teachers. And you brought us the Bible—and brought it in a way we could understand it!' They begged us to set up an Oral Bible School on their island. We said 'Yes.'"

Two weeks later the school began.

Three months into the school, we received a surprising report from our director. (By then, the twelve students would have learned and discussed 60 stories.) Our director reported, "Although we do not know which stories God used to bring the students to make a change, the pastors in this region decided polygamy is wrong. They covenanted to stop taking on multiple wives. As well, they agreed that to honor Scripture, the pastors with more than one wife must step down."

Since then, these precious believers have stayed true to their commitment.

After their one-year school finished, and the twelve students graduated, they went on to establish another OBS.

As well, the man who had originally invited the instructors to come lead that first workshop gave this remarkable testimony at an OBS graduation:

> I tried for three years to influence the Africa STS Director. We needed money for our orphanage and I was thinking that with his western connections he would surely help me.
>
> Well we came together last year, but he gave no money! Instead, his team taught me and our fellow believers on Lake Victoria Island how to learn from God's Word!
>
> I am now happy to report that as of last week, all 70 orphans have support. And it is our transformed community that supports our own orphans.

[We looked with awe at the radical reformation in a whole community. As people listened to God's Word with understanding, they responded with repentance and change of a deeply-held custom. They demonstrated love for the helpless and even the use of their own funds was affected. A true "doer of the Word" is described in James 1:27. "Pure religion and undefiled before God and the Father is this, To visit the fatherless and widows in their affliction, and to keep himself unspotted from the world." That verse perfectly describes the moral change of these islanders and their actions toward the orphans.]

Graduates Carry On

As funds allow, each OBS graduate receives this gift of a solar player. After graduation most continue as pastors, teachers, and evangelists. In addition to those areas of ministry, about 25% of them choose to serve as overseers in new Oral Bible Schools and serve as STS instructors. Instructors serve as unpaid volunteers. When called for and needed, TGSP pays for low cost travel and food for instructors and overseers. Sometimes a small honorarium will be paid to those in need.

Regional Empowerment

One country director received an invitation to minister in schools throughout his nation. Besides already being involved in school ministry, the STS staff in this country was actively leading workshops and overseeing OBSs. That invitation prompted us to develop Regional Empowerment, which is a plan to efficiently and effectively use funds, time and staff.

This strategy for each region is combining ministry, workshops and an OBS. A region includes an average of 25 different villages. To accomplish this, three instructors go to a region three different times over a nine month period. After those three trainings, one instructor continues visiting the region's newly established OBS. The instructor visits monthly over the next eleven months in order to encourage and oversee the OBS.

The empowerment includes gift copies of *God's Story*, solar players with Bible content and training, and other resources. Because each trip serves multiple purposes, the cost for the instructor's travel and food is very small. The number of people impacted in a region is often over 2,500. After the visits are completed, local leaders will have been trained and equipped— empowered from then on to lead and minister utilizing the Bible in understood and applicable ways.

Chapter 9: Pulling Out the Quills – Paradigm Shifts in Thinking

Pulling Out the Quills: Struggle of Adopting Oral Strategies

The porcupine defends itself by embedding its quills (spines) in animals that threaten it. Its sharp quills go in easily but, due to a small barb on the quill, pulling them out is painful.

The "pulling out of the quills" we refer to in the title of this chapter is not the taking away of time-tested successful methods of preaching and teaching. Quills are the beliefs that:

- You cannot effectively teach without notes.

- You must use information from outside a passage.

- You cannot teach deeply outside of traditional techniques.

- The uneducated cannot study the Bible inductively.

It continues to be our experience that at first, people will struggle with many of the tenants of STS. Those with education, especially theological training, struggle more than do the oral learners.

To experience full effectiveness, we encourage those seriously trying to learn STS to fully try each of the concepts. But getting seasoned, educated pastors and leaders to try some of these new experiences, such as not taking notes, is a bit like pulling out those imbedded porcupine quills! We pull. The learners yell, "Ouch!" But when the quill is out, the learners show amazement and joy as they see they have gained an added skill that actually does work!

Traditional Presentation Compared to STS Style

The Usual Methods of Teaching From a Story. When using traditional styles of preaching and teaching, usually a passage or story is read, and then verse-by-verse exposition is done. Sometimes the passage is not even read; the speaker just goes directly to verse-by-verse teaching. Then the verses read are referenced as a platform from which to teach. Additional Scriptures are also brought in to emphasize certain truths.

Sometimes information from outside the Bible will be presented, and then maybe some Greek or Hebrew word meanings will be mentioned to support the speaker's points. Occasionally a bit of humor or a story may be brought into the sermon to keep people engaged.

If applications to the listeners are made, those applications are usually woven into the sermon as it is delivered or they are tacked on at the end. Note that the applications are made by the teacher. The applications are given in the form of telling the listeners what they should or should not do. This customary style of presentation is certainly not wrong. However, these methods of presentation are not the *only* ways to teach the passage.

STS Style. By contrast, when a person teaches using STS, listeners are assisted in discovering spiritual information from the Bible. Pastors whose hearts have longed to see their congregations take an active role in studying the Bible, love seeing the joy on the people's faces when they discover for themselves something new in the Word of God!

One highly literate pastor and leader in reaching international students in the US attended an STS workshop. This accomplished author now weaves STS into his ministry. He wrote:

> The difference between this [STS] approach and a more literate approach is that, with the former, we treat the Bible less as a book to be deciphered and dissected, and more as a record of events lived out in the framework of historical reality. In this [STS] framework, we begin to see events as live, with undercurrents of parallel realities (such as the emotions of the people involved, the spiritual connections, etc.) to be discovered along the way.

As we introduce *Simply The Story* around the world, we observe this recurring response: Usually, the least educated acquire most of the STS skills more quickly than the highly educated. Does this mean that the least educated of the world are smarter than educated people? Of course not!

We Do Recognize This. When people have studied a certain system, and have used it with some degree of success, learning a new system that seems to be in opposition to what they already know, presents a huge challenge. As stated, the highly educated usually struggle the most with utilizing all of the parts of the STS process.

The main reason for this imbalance is easy to detect. Although nearly all of the highly educated Christians who attend STS workshops give hearty mental assent to STS, when they venture out to learn Scripture and present it in an oral style, that new approach feels strange. The methods they have been taught, and upon which they have built their ministries, are not oral. So their first reaction to the multiple new components is to employ only some of the new parts of the process.

Areas of discomfort include:

- Letting go of collating parallel passages.
- Learning without any notes.
- Teaching without notes.
- Confining a presentation to just one passage.
- Not bringing in any outside information.
- Leading to truths through discussion as opposed to lecture.
- Presenting a story without reading it aloud to learners (or with minimal reading).
- Trusting a story to stand alone.
- Letting multiple topics be discovered during discussion. Believing that discovery will be what is taught by the teacher and also what develops during the discussion.

Important to Note. We definitely do not consider any of those familiar techniques to be wrong or in need of being discarded. But with the rising awareness of the high percentage of people in the world who need to be reached though oral strategies, we see the importance of helping people expand into newer and even more effective teaching styles. We celebrate the interest Christian pastors and educators are showing in expanding their repertoire of Scripture presentations to include the oral strategy of STS.

Both of the following reports (one from Thailand and one from Nigeria) demonstrate answers to many of the areas of discomfort on the list above and, in general, they show the importance of incorporating oral strategies.

A youth worker in Thailand observed:

> I am quite used to preparing lesson objectives and starting my lessons with a clear objective. And I always make sure to reinforce that objective throughout the lesson and even tack it on at the conclusion to make sure my listeners don't miss it. However, fairly soon after teaching a lesson, my listeners don't seem to remember it.
>
> With STS there is always a clear objective that runs parallel to my typical objectives, but the big difference is that I find listeners are able to discover my objective on their own as they answer my questions. Discovering it for themselves seals it to their hearts and minds and as a result they have long range retention of what I wanted to teach.

Nobody But God Would Pick That Story.

Some very conscientious Christian leaders have expressed concern about confining teaching to only one story at a time. They are especially cautious about using a story passage apart from other Scriptures. For example, we were once asked, "Will the listeners be shown how each of the Bible stories is a part of God's great redemptive plan and points forward to Jesus' work on the cross? (See Luke 24:27 and Acts 8:35.) When separated from the big picture Story of Scripture (the gospel), Bible stories quickly become no more than lessons teaching moral behavior."

We would respond to this thoughtful concern in several ways. The enemies of the Cross will always try to lower Jesus, ignore mankind's utter helplessness and God's redemptive plan. Of those deceptions, we are acutely aware.

We find the answer to this staying-in-one-story question in the ability and role of the Holy Spirit. He will speak His message out of a story even without the storyteller-teacher preselecting the topic or preaching a point to people. This occurs over and over as we use discussion to deeply and seriously unpack all that is in a story.

When the lecture-style delivery of Scripture is used, the format does not allow the teacher to detect who is ready to hear how to be saved, so, of necessity, the invitation goes out to everyone. But STS discussion-style teaching enables the storyteller to talk with people. A group "conversation" about spiritual things takes place.

During the conversation, whenever there is interest in knowing more about God, or in how to know Jesus, storytellers can respond to the specific need. The storyteller can provide a direct gospel presentation and the Scriptures that would reveal God's redemptive plan whenever led to do so. How the Holy Spirit speaks to people through Scripture and draws people to salvation is demonstrated in this next report.

Five STS workshops were done in east and north Nigeria. Three months later, the instructor returned to Nigeria to see "if they got it." Since during the training all that was being taught was being translated into four languages, he was not sure.

"Not only did they get it," he reported, "they practice it, and they use it!"

One evangelist told the STS instructor that he had led nine Muslim men to the Lord. The evangelist shared what it was that reached these men. He reported that the new believers said, "We knew of the people in the stories but the Koran does not tell us the whole story and no one ever discusses with us."

100

When asked what story was told that touched them, the evangelist said, "It was Moses and the Rock. You know, in Exodus 17."

As a senior instructor of STS, this report surprised me. I asked, "But what was it in that story that reached them?"

The STS instructor related:

> The evangelist told me that the new believers said, "When we heard the story and talked about it, we saw that Moses was a faithful leader, but the people were disrespectful to Moses. We were amazed that Moses went to God and asked what to do with the people. Moses cared for the people! Our leaders don't care for us. And God didn't punish the people. He gave them water. He showed mercy. We want to know that God."

I thought to myself: *Would I have selected that story of Moses for evangelism? Would that story have been on my list as a good one for Muslims?* No, it would not have been selected - well, at least not selected before I started learning how people who yearn for God will be drawn to God throughout His Word—including stories.

Regardless of whether or not that story would have been on my list, it was on the Holy Spirit's list! We see this again and again in the use of STS. When God's Word is delivered whole, as He wrote it, and when its treasures are discovered by listeners through discussion, supernatural power is unleashed!

We encourage those who use that Exodus 17 story to consider telling another story right after it. The listeners would have discussed the way God provided life-giving water out of a rock. So, their eyes widen in awe when they hear the next story found in 1 Corinthians 10:1-6. They grasp the importance of the part that describes that past event of the rock and water. "And did all drink the same spiritual drink: for they drank of that spiritual Rock that followed them: and that Rock was Christ." The people recognize the typology in that new story; they see the picture of Jesus!

Talk about a redemptive theme! Those two stories, one after the other, graphically show God's plan. But was it that second story with the typology that spoke to those Muslim men? No, it wasn't. Did you notice in the report from Nigeria what it was in the Moses story that drew those nine men to ask how they could know God? Yes. It was the tangible evidence of God's mercy and the men wanting to know that God of mercy. So, of course, the evangelist, who had just told the Moses story, happily explained to those men the way of faith. He told them how they could know God through His Son, Jesus Christ.

What About the Epistles?

But, when considering this paradigm shift of teaching Bible by using its stories wrapped in oral methods, many who love all of God's Word, and who know that the whole council of God is relevant, ask this excellent question: "What about the Epistles?" We offer numerous responses for consideration.

One Is This. For a long time the stories of the Bible have been dissected, disassembled, and used just as springboards to illustrate topical sermons. Unfortunately, to be understood and remembered by oral learners, these stories needed to be heard intact as they were written.

Certainly, if through the incorporation of oral strategies and use of stories, 75% of the Bible can be clearly understood by 80% of the world who previously may not have understood our presentations—that should be cause for celebration!

We are encouraged as Christian educators, pastors and missionaries are discovering this biblical and powerful way to teach and preach. The effectiveness of STS goes beyond theory. Those who venture out and try presenting stories in their wholeness and discussing them in depth, in this oral, inductive way, are seeing verifiable, positive results.

The hearty response to the *Simply The Story* style of teaching Bible stories was evidenced by the number of places utilizing it in its first six years. STS had been introduced or was being used in 90 nations.

An example of the fast growth came to us. We led three workshops in the Philippines. Afterward, a host sent us this note. "Four months later I contacted a number of these people [attendees] and found 1,400 people had already been trained and STS was being taught in 25 languages!"

A Wycliffe translator learned STS in the USA. She sent a few of her village leaders to that workshop in the Philippines for added training. Four months later, five Filipinos they had trained led a workshop in the city. The Wycliffe translator wrote, "The educated pastors asked, 'When can you come back and teach us more?' The pastors had no idea that three of those instructors who trained them were nonliterates!"

Newly empowered oral learners, many of whom are nonliterate, are demonstrating their comprehension by aggressively sharing stories with others. We thrill at hearing multiple reports of 5th and 6th generation replication of told and taught stories—inside of one year! The wealth of spiritual fruit we see is a testimony to the power of God's Word when wrapped in its original "packaging"—the story.

Ah, But Still … What About The Epistles?

The basic principles of STS can be applied to any section of the Bible.

We demonstrate in workshops how some passages from the Epistles can easily be presented using 100% of the STS format. We often include a story from the Epistles and Psalms for presentation and demonstration. These sections of the Bible are a bit less recognizable as stories, but we show that many sections within the Epistles, books of poetry, and the Prophets are visual and have a discernible storyline. As such, they can be presented quite effectively using STS.

If you are familiar with the five-verse chapter of Psalm 1, close your eyes and use the *Wise Counsellor* questions to see what the two kinds of men in Psalm 1 are doing. Look carefully at their choices, what they could have chosen and the results and impact of their choices. Notice how God is interacting in their lives and what you see of the character of God.

Again, close your eyes to consider another familiar passage. See in your mind the sweet and personal way the sheep-narrator of Psalm 23 describes his shepherd. (You can hear much more than we told you earlier in the story of Ramesh and the 23rd Psalm.) Listen well to that sheep. After you see the whole story, only then go back and ask application questions from what you observed in the story. What could apply to us as sheep-people today and to the Shepherd, Jesus?

Try looking at the storyline in Isaiah 1:10-20, Romans 1:14-25 and James 1:22-27. Admittedly, those passages are more challenging to remember than a standard story, which has dialog and people experiencing an episode of life. Go slowly. Notice what the characters are saying and doing. Do they make choices? Are there results and impact of those choices?

Clearly in those passages, God reveals His character in multiple ways. Make use of the STS principles. Try confining your discovery of Spiritual Observations to just what is seen in the story. After this is completed, go back to the beginning of the "story" and consider how all those observation you found apply to us today.

Throughout the Bible we find three types of passages:

- Story passages.
- Semistory passages.
- Nonstory passages.

The story passages are definitely the easiest of the three types to remember.

Story passages can be seen with the mind's eye. Stories are events that took place in the material world. They are interactive and have characters, action and dialog. As a result, stories can be experienced along with the characters; they can be seen—and heard—and felt.

Semistory passages are a bit more challenging to learn. Although they are less of a story per se, they do have visual sections in them, so we can remember what we "see" as well as what we hear. Semistory passages contain less interaction and are likely to be monologs or descriptive in content. Much within the books of the Prophets fits this semistory category. Examples of semistories would be Psalm 1, Romans 11 and James.

The most difficult passages to remember are the nonstory passages, because they are the least visual of the three. They tend to be instructional monologs, often topical in nature. Many sections of the Epistles would be considered nonstory passages.

Even though the Epistles consist, for the most part, of nonstory passages, they can still be presented and taught by making use of most of the STS techniques. Well-told stories captivate listeners. The Epistles are passionate letters, written by passionate people from a passionate God. During presentation, teachers must recognize this passion and read or speak those words to others with that passion.

In ministry, one way to handle hard-to-remember, nonstory passages is to read them aloud and then use STS principles to teach them.

Perhaps this dilemma of how to teach nonstory passages in an oral way can be solved by covering only a few verses at a time. Teaching only a few verses at a time is done very often in standard expository preaching. Those few verses, if told with feeling and discussed afterwards in chronological order, can be remembered by listeners. The challenge is to confine yourself to just those verses and, perhaps, to a small introduction of Bible information that will place the passage in context.

Can this be done? Will you have enough to talk about without going to many other passages in the Bible (or even to sources outside the Bible) to "shed light" on the text?

Yes, it can be done and we demonstrate this in workshops.

From one very short passage we demonstrate the richness of God's Word. First we tell a small introduction to give the listeners context and prior biblical information needed to develop and discuss the story. We say, "Jesus was speaking His last words to His disciples in Jerusalem, the city that would become the 'headquarters' of the early church. These disciples had traveled for three years with Jesus in many places including the larger region of Judea and even in the neighboring region of Samaria where despised people lived."

Then we tell our "story," found in Acts 1:8. Yes, we tell a one-verse-long story in STS. Due to how much can be found and discussed there, we only cover the last half of that verse! This story can easily fill 30 minutes. People seasoned in the Word, and those new to the Bible, all heartily join in the discussion. Amazing discoveries and even tearful applications are made. What's more, people leave with ownership and understanding of the passage so that they can, and do, share the story with others.

Pastors and Christian educators must seriously ponder this possibility: The lecture and preaching style of presentation most commonly used in Christendom may not be the most effective way to deliver the biblical truths that they want people to learn and act upon. At a minimum, Bible communicators should consider incorporating some interactive, listener-discovery methods of delivery into Christian teaching.

Some who use "story" wisely are introducing passages from the Epistles as they teach through the book of Acts. As these pastors and teachers teach interactively through the stories of Acts, they bring in the Epistles that tie in with the missionary trips referenced in Acts. The general principles that make STS effective, asking questions and using interactive discussion to find Spiritual Observations and Spiritual Applications, also work well when applied to the Epistles as they are taught.

Most often, it is highly-literate presenters who train pastors and teachers. If these highly-literate educators are not familiar with the dynamics of an oral presentation of Scripture, how can they teach people who want to minister to oral learners and those who cannot read? Do nonreaders deserve to understand the nonstory passages? If so, can those who are highly literate, and who most probably highly intelligent, use their giftedness to figure out how to train those who are less trained and gifted?

What About the Importance of Memorizing Scripture Word for Word?

Two thoughts come to mind. One being the vital need and biblical injunction to "hide God's Word in our hearts," and the other, taking an objective look at memorization and remembering.

By God's grace, many believers have been involved in Bible memory programs. These programs emphasize word for word memorization along with the verse reference. Those of us who have memorized many

Scriptures, especially at a young age, when we had agile minds, will forever be grateful for that regimen. We benefited greatly.

But, the challenges of Scripture memorization are these: few attain a substantial quantity of verses this way and retaining these verses long-term requires constant drilling. However, you can learn a story by remembering it, as we have outlined in this book and, if you retell it a few times, you will find that you need very little or no review after that. The story remains graphically in your memory and, since it is retained in your own words, it is natural and easy to repeat.

In a 33-hour STS workshop, attendees hear and actively discuss at least 21 different stories. As stated, when a story is reviewed and told several times, it can be accurately told and remembered for a lifetime! These 21 workshop stories contain 148 verses!

Amazing! Learning and storing 148 verses in one's "heart pocket" and being able to naturally speak them "in season and out of season" would put a person far ahead of most Christians in their ability to speak the Bible.

Memorizing and Remembering. Compare pages of Bibles that are written in various languages. Do they look the same? Are the words anything alike? No. In fact, they may even utilize differing scripts and alphabets to present their words. The words look entirely different, and the spoken words sound completely different, but they have something in common. That commonality is what should be the same in every Bible. What is it? Yes. It is the concepts, the information, not the exact words. The message does not change, even though the words are completely different.

In STS we caution everyone to be extremely careful not to add to, subtract from or alter the exact content of the story by careless selection of words, voice inflection or actions. We encourage people to tell Bible stories in a conversational way. But extreme importance is placed on not changing concepts or information, no matter how small or unimportant that information may seem to be.

Memorization has been and always will be a vital tool for internalizing the Word of God. But precise remembering of stories and passages, and speaking them conversationally, belongs in our memory tool chest as well.

Can the Uneducated Study the Bible Inductively?

Sometimes people assume that those who are literate are also skilled at critical thinking. And conversely, the assumption is that those who are not literate (or who come from oral communication backgrounds) are not, and never will be, logical or inductive thinkers.

Certainly, discussion of these premises needs to be continued. Perhaps definitions of critical thinking and logical, inductive and deductive reasoning, and their role in learning, need to be more clearly defined and understood—particularly as they relate to oral learners.

From a biblical perspective, can we conclude that the ability to think critically is bestowed only upon the educated or, even more narrowly, only upon those who are educated and whose cultural roots are literate?

That conclusion loses credibility when we consider that all people are created in the image of God (Gen. 1:26-27). And, as such, all people are endowed with the gift of reason and rationality and have, since the Fall, had conscience for moral reasoning, even when they reject that reason. (Romans 1:19-23).

It is interesting to note in Mark 12:24, when the highly educated Sadducees approached Jesus with a question designed to trap him, that He responded back to them with a question, "Do ye not therefore err, because ye know not the scriptures, neither the power of God?"

We know that the religious Sadducees "knew" the words of the Scriptures, so Jesus seems here to be referring to the Sadducee's lack of discerning the spiritual meaning of the words. Because these religious leaders lacked spiritual discernment, they missed vital information, so their critical thinking and deductive skills failed to bring them truth.

As mentioned before, we see Scripture as supracultural. Storytellers using STS find that as long as they provide any needed explanations in the introductions, multiple treasures in the Bible stories can be discovered by listeners worldwide—regardless of their education or reading ability.

We are reminded in Acts 4:13 of the educational background of at least some of the disciples Jesus selected. It seems that Peter and John had angered the Sadducees and other religious leaders by their strong preaching about Jesus. So those religious leaders had the two arrested and then brought them in front of their council to answer questions. Peter, led by the Holy Spirit, gave a logical and well ordered speech about the religious leaders and about Jesus, a speech that cornered their highly educated captors.

The men on the council were affected by Peter's speech:

> Now when they saw the boldness of Peter and John, and perceived that they were unlearned and ignorant men, they marvelled; and they took knowledge of them, that they had been with Jesus. (Acts 4:13)

Does this happen today? Can unlearned followers of Jesus listen well to Scripture and then logically discover and teach others many deep truths?

Reports From the Field Might Help Answer this Question

God's Word Speaks to the Hidden Parts of the Heart.
Sometimes western STS instructors have opportunities to use STS in rural settings or to see it used there. A village that a few of us westerners visited in Kenya was Ekalakala. Previously, the African STS instructors had ministered to them using stories and had started training them in STS.

Our guide explained, "When we first came here, 'church' was singing, clapping, preaching and maybe one Scripture verse—that was it! The believers knew very little about the Bible. Now these pastors are seeing salvations and growth."

Join Us in What We Saw. You enter a cement block, tin-roofed, village church in Ekalakala. You see that it is filled with about 60 people from the Kamba tribe. Among those on the church benches are 15 pastors, representing 11 different churches, waiting for the program to begin.

You notice the women's colorful dresses and hats and the men wearing their finest coats and ties. As you focus in, you see that most of the coats look several sizes too large and hang loosely on these slender-framed people. Then you notice frayed sleeves and trousers worn thin. You think, *Who knows how many different people have used these same "Sunday clothes."*

You are told that the teaching must end by 4:00 pm so that the people can cross the river to return home before the hippos come out. As well, you discover that most in the church face a four-hour walk to reach their homes—round, mud huts.

While there, an African prepares to tell Genesis 35:1-5 and to lead a discussion on it. This presentation will be done in Swahili and translated into Kamba. After you sit down on a back bench, your African translator begins to tell you in English what is taking place.

"The people discussed how Jacob had been protected by God for a long time and that God is now calling Jacob and his family to go back to Bethel, the place Jacob had met God.

"They are now talking about how Jacob is a good spiritual leader who is making his family clean themselves and get rid of their idols. They just called Jacob 'obedient to God.'

"The storyteller just asked the people, 'Do you see Jacob as just now becoming a good leader in this story or has he been a godly leader for a long time?' And then he asked, 'Do you think what Jacob did with the idols might show you anything?'

The people seemed to be debating with each other.

A few minutes later, your translator whispers to you, "Now they are seeing more in the story. They said, 'Jacob gathered all of the idols held by his family and then hid those pagan objects under THE oak tree in Shechem! He marked the spot!' Now they're talking about Jacob's greed. 'He didn't trust God for supply!

"'He is a compromiser to have let his family keep idols,' they are saying. "A man just said, 'Some of the occult items were earrings, so Jacob must have known before about idols being in his house.'"

As those gathered in the church discuss Jacob's actions, one lady stands up and excitedly gestures and points while rapidly saying something in Kamba.

Your interpreter whispers, "The lady is saying, 'We are Christians now, but we still have our charms and sacred objects hidden away. We must not hide them anymore. We must destroy them!'"

Then a few minutes later a big man stands and booms something loudly, to which the rest of the men respond in agreement.

By now you are dying to know what is being said, so you quickly lean over to your interpreter and prompt, "What is he saying?"

The interpreter waits to hear all the man is saying and then whispers back, "This man just said, 'I rule my family. They do as I tell them. But I am like Jacob. I have not led them spiritually. I must change.'"

[That day, in that Bible story, all in the church discovered Jacob's hypocrisy. Both the man and the woman, who stood and spoke, recognized their own sins as they looked at Jacob's sins.

Also that day, we witnessed the supernatural power of God's stories to speak messages to the center of people's worldview! These mostly uneducated oral communicators found deep truth and made the kind of personal applications that may take missionaries scores of years, praying and seeking, to witness.]

Never Too Late, Never too Lost.

In the Nawalparasi district of Nepal lived a witchdoctor who, in all of his 66 years, had never learned to read—but he controlled hundreds of people, people who looked up to him in awe and in fear.

Starting in his 60s, this man had heard about Jesus, but he thought that he didn't need Jesus. Sure, he had heard reports about people who had prayed in Jesus' name and their prayers had been answered. But the spirits had helped this witchdoctor, so why would he need Jesus' help?

One day his grandson became very sick, near-to-death sick. The witchdoctor chanted and begged the spirits to heal the boy, but the boy was still dying. Finally, in desperation, the old man went to the Jesus followers and asked them to pray for his grandson. They prayed, and the sickness left the boy. But the old man did not become a follower of Jesus and continued his life as a witchdoctor.

About three months later, this man's wife, who was a believer, attended an STS workshop. That evening she returned home and told her husband a story she had just learned.

The story of Naaman from 2 Kings 5 had been taught by Nepalis and discussed by the attendees. They had learned that Naaman was the captain of the Syrian army and that he had leprosy. And then, although Syria was an enemy of Israel, when Naaman heard that he could be healed by a prophet in Israel, he had assembled a big caravan and traveled to Israel to seek that healing.

But, when Naaman went to the prophet Elisha's home, Elisha did not meet Naaman's expectations. In fact, the prophet did not even come out to greet Naaman! And when a servant came out instead and delivered the prophet's instructions to go dip in a local river seven times to be healed, Naaman responded, "Are not Abana and Pharpar, rivers of Damascus, better than all the waters of Israel? May I not wash in them, and be clean?" So he turned and went away in a rage.

It was only after Naaman's servants begged him to go and do this humble act and dip in the river to try for a healing that Naaman complied. He went to the river, dipped as he had been told—and was instantly healed!

When this witchdoctor heard this story, he said to his wife, "I am Naaman. My pride is stopping me from following Jesus."

The next day the witchdoctor went to the workshop with his wife. There he told an instructor, "I want to be a follower of Jesus." He was counseled, and he then prayed for salvation. Afterwards, this uneducated old man, who had spent most of his life in the world of the occult, asked if he could tell those gathered what had just happened. This was his speech:

"Naaman was a proud man and nearly lost his healing because of that pride. I, too, am a proud man. I knew for years that I should follow Jesus, but I didn't want to admit that I needed Him. People looked up to me. I didn't want to lose my position, even when God healed my grandson. My pride nearly cost me my salvation! But now—I am now a follower of Jesus."

Surely, when anyone, educated or not, discovers spiritual information in the Bible, the Holy Spirit must first receive credit. But we do see that after the ex-witchdoctor listened to a Bible story, he used inductive thinking skills and saw his own decisions mirrored in that story. The depth of that discovery transcended education.

Interestingly, in those field reports, the people who ministered and led the workshops were 2nd, 3rd and 4th generation, indigenous STS instructors. All came from oral communication cultures and most were originally from villages.

What About the Use of Commentaries?

Commentaries offer a wealth of wisdom to those who study Scripture. Christians through the ages have benefited, not just from the spoken insights that godly men and women have shared, but also from the legacy of written insights they have left behind. In some way, investigating the view of a commentator is much like listening to someone give an opinion in person. But one subtle difference in our acceptance of information can be this. We tend to expect published teaching to be particularly accurate. Time, study and usually some kind of oversight go into published work. However, no matter the source, whether it is people's opinions or written information, both must be verified by Scripture.

The Lord showed us how to substantiate what is taught to us:

> And the brethren immediately sent away Paul and Silas by night unto Berea... These were more noble than those in Thessalonica, in that they received the word with all readiness of mind, and searched the scriptures daily, whether those things were so. (Acts 17:10-11)

These people in the city of Berea were complimented for measuring the validity of what they were being taught by the Scriptures. The Bereans held up the Scriptures as their final authority. Interesting! I wonder whose teachings were being measured for validity? You are correct! The Apostle Paul's!

So today, following that example, we must use the Bible to measure information presented to us in whatever form it comes—in person, in commentaries or in other teaching material.

When ministering through story to people who have access to recorded or written Scripture, at the end of your discussion, be sure to provide listeners with the Scripture reference of your story. This will allow your listeners to confirm the accuracy of what you have taught and discussed with them.

At a large gathering in Africa, everyone was lauding the effectiveness of stories and the STS oral approach. One eager (and slightly opportunistic) young man who was learning Bible stories asked an interesting question. He ventured, "Can you send us commentaries?" At first I was taken aback, but then responded, "That might be arranged," I smiled. "Contact us when you have learned all of the 210 stories we've listed. That way you will be prepared to measure the validity of the information in the commentaries."

In some circles, the opinions of commentators have been elevated to a position higher than the plain sense of the Scriptures themselves. Sometimes people take their understanding of the Word from commentators because they lack motivation to study on their own. Rather than taking time to dig in and learn from the Bible, these people just incorporate, as truth, the views of educated and published theologians.

All of us must guard against the mindset that, although the Bible is for the common person, the deepest and richest truths it contains can only be understood by educated theologians, either those who preach in our churches or those who write their findings for others. God's desire is for all people to have access to His truth, not just an elite few who happen to have been blessed with a formal education.

In a sense, participating in a group discussion about a Bible story is like enjoying valuable information that writers provide in commentaries. During the discussion, whenever someone offers a view about the story that may or may not be valid, we feel free to ask, "Now where do you see that in the story?" In the same way, we encourage everyone to authenticate information in commentaries by asking the same question.

Actually, when anyone gives a suggestion as to the meaning of a passage, they are in effect serving in the role of a commentator. Therefore, no matter who is offering a view, whether it is a beginner in the Word or a highly educated theologian who is sharing the fruit of many years of study, be sure that what is shared is clearly seen inside that Bible story.

Chapter 10: Classifications of *Simply The Story* Storytellers

Practitioner. During all workshops, attendees receive training and personal coaching. Our responsibility and joy is to hand off information on how to do STS. Learners then need to practice the STS concepts and fine-tune their skills.

A person who has attended an STS workshop is a "practitioner." From that exposure, most attendees are able to utilize the STS concepts well enough to go to their circles of influence and effectively tell Bible stories and deliver truths through discussion. We strongly encourage and urge the practitioners to go out and tell the Bible stories. We even offer various materials that practitioners can use for incremental handing off of STS methods.

While practitioners are prepared to become active storytellers, they are NOT yet ready to lead an STS workshop or to formally train others under the STS name.

Sometimes we are asked by people who lead ministries if it is a good plan to weave the teaching of STS in with their other teaching material. We respond by applauding the principle of that idea. Practitioners can vision cast. They can easily inform and enthuse people about STS. They can combine what they now know with targeted information we can give them for vision casting. We love seeing that take place.

Our caution is this. To properly teach STS, one needs to:

- Have a firm understanding of every part of the STS process.

- Be able to demonstrate a clear STS model.

- Know the apologetics (purpose and use) of all that defines STS.

Some practitioners might want to run ahead of being completely trained and becoming certified as instructors because "they want to keep it simple and quickly get this new information out to those who need it."

A few times, we have seen enthusiastic, well-meaning practitioners set up and lead unauthorized STS trainings. But, because those doing that training were not fully trained as STS instructors, they were not yet able to provide a fully formed STS training. The resulting buy-in by those they instructed was small. But what is worse, those who had come to this training with the expectation of learning an effective, reproducible model of teaching and discussing stories, did not receive a complete or satisfying experience.

Those attendees left half prepared, and what is worse, they mistakenly thought that they had just received the full "STS experience." As a result of the early, weak exposure, they rarely are interested in attending a fully authorized STS workshop, because they think they have already tasted STS, and it did not work that well for them. Sadly, we never get the opportunity to teach them the full set of skills.

"Simply" is Not Simple. At a glance, the name *"Simply The Story"* might lead people to think that STS is "simple" and that it only involves telling a story. If that is all we did in a workshop, we could easily accomplish the training in one day! But actually, what STS imparts involves multiple paradigm shifts in teaching and mission strategy.

As well, there are added paradigm shifts both on a personal level and in ministry application in how people learn and how most effectively to communicate biblical information to others.

Considering that those who lead workshops have invested a great deal of time and practice to be able to generate such enthusiasm in the practitioners, we ask that practitioners who want to effectively teach make that same investment.

Without proper training in how to train others in STS, the next generation of storytellers will end up with less than adequate training. When those people struggle with using stories in ministry, that disappointment can cause them to mistakenly decide that storytelling does not work and give it up all together.

The initial 5-day training is how to do and use STS and how to start on the road to training others. That training does not include how to lead an STS workshop, how to do diagnostic coaching nor the purposes and apologetics for the many paradigm shifts in the STS process and methods.

Does this mean that practitioners cannot be involved in multiplying disciples and helping others learn and use STS skills? Not at all! In fact, we encourage this sort of handing off of STS in a discipleship setting. For more information on Discipleship Multiplication, see the information in this handbook, Chapter 12: Places to Use – Ways to Learn STS.

If you want to see your group trained, please contact us. We'd be glad to work with you. And, if you desire, we would love to map out a plan to bring you to full instructor status. Our specialty is in handing off leadership in a thorough manner. People can become certified instructors as quickly as they: know the workshop content, show proficiency in telling STS stories, know the reason and purpose for each of the elements of

STS training, show their ability at diagnostic coaching and demonstrate to a senior instructor their ability to lead a workshop using the STS guidelines.

Instructors: Assistant, Provisional, Certified and Senior

To fit into any of these instructor classifications we want the staff to be of one mind and heart in the essentials of the faith. We ask that the prospective instructors agree to the TGSP-STS Doctrinal Statement below (also on our website).

Doctrinal Statement

We adhere to the following truths:

- The divine inspiration of the whole Old and New Testament, the only book inspired by God.
- The doctrine of the Trinity.
- The fall of man, his consequent moral depravity and his need for regeneration.
- The deity and humanity of Jesus Christ, His virgin birth, sinless life, substitutionary and atoning death, bodily resurrection, ascension into heaven, future bodily return to the earth.
- The doctrine of justification by faith alone, in Christ alone.
- The resurrection of the body, both of the just and the unjust.
- The eternal life of the saved and the eternal punishment of the lost.

Assistant Instructors. After attending a workshop, most Practitioners qualify to assist as small group 'tribe' leaders in an STS workshop as Assistant Instructors.

Provisional Instructors. After a minimum of three days of assisting in a workshop, Assistant Instructors who wish to advance need to be able to clearly explain the process of preparation and presentation. They must also show an ability to kindly, wisely and gently teach STS to others. A Certified Instructor may approve and give the Provisional Instructor title to those who qualify.

Certified Instructors. After assisting in one or more workshops, Provisional Instructors may apply for Certified Instructor status. Applicants need to be able to demonstrate to a Senior Instructor specific skill levels in all parts of an STS workshop and STS concepts.

Certified Instructors may run official STS workshops in all leadership roles except approving others as Certified Instructors.

Senior Instructors. To be considered for Senior Instructor status, a Certified Instructor must first teach alongside a Senior Instructor and show expertise at teaching, evaluating and encouraging new storytellers, and be able to organize and lead workshops.

Senior Instructors not only may lead STS workshops, but they are the only people who can approve and grant "Certified Instructor" status to qualified Provisional Instructors.

Instructors for the STS Oral Bible Schools, currently being led in multiple countries, come from the pool of indigenous Certified Instructors.

Chapter 11: Places to Use –
Ways to Learn and Spread STS

Places to Use *Simply The Story*

Fold STS Into Your Existing Ministry. Whether you work with children, teenagers, young adults or adults of any age, STS will enliven discussion and involve your people in the study of God's Word.

By adjusting the number of observations and applications you cover, you can tailor the length of the story presentation to whatever time you have available. If you have a limited time, say less than 30 minutes, you can save a bit of time by leaving out step 2 of Presentation Phase One. Do not have a volunteer retell the story. You tell the story. Then you lead the group through the story by asking them to retell it together. The STS model will still work.

Conversational STS. When the allotted time or opportunity to tell an STS story is extremely short, you can do some very creative things. In trainings, after people grasp the basics of STS, we coach them in this very practical application of STS. Briefly, this is how it is done:

A story can be told in just over a minute and a few selected observations and applications can be done in 5 to 10 minutes. Tell the story, and then go right to a few selected observations and then their applications. Before you ask each question, repeat the part of the story in detail that contains the treasure you want people to discover.

If, for example, you were telling the story in Mark 1:40-45, you could say, "Remember how Jesus felt compassion when the leper bowed down and begged Jesus and said 'If you will, you can make me clean.'?" This is the key. Ask a question that includes enough detail to remind people of the story they just heard, so that they can respond well to your question.

Pastors Innovate. Pastors of traditional and conservative denominations and congregations usually hesitate to use STS from the pulpit. It is just not customary in most churches for a pastor to ask questions during a sermon. Additionally, to tell a story instead of reading it is a big leap in some circles. Pastors from around the world who have attended STS workshops and liked the concept have found these solutions:

1. Various pastors have reported to us about using STS in informal youth meetings. The responses were very positive from the youth. Afterwards, the parents came to the pastors and said such things as, "Why don't you teach us this way?"

2. Other pastors use the STS style from the pulpit. Except, instead of telling the story, they read the story from Scripture. They also move from a conservative, formal way of reading to an animated interesting style. They tell it "storytelling" style.

Afterwards, they ask the Spiritual Observation and Application questions. Some encouraged audible responses; others ask rhetorical questions, which allows people time to process the question and think about a response in their minds. That is vital. Those pastors must make certain to give people the time they need to think about what they would answer.

3. Some showcase STS as "A way that those far from us who cannot read are being reached." The positive responses to this way of presenting the Bible to "others" opens the door to use a customized form of STS in their churches.

4. Some pastors introduce STS to their Sunday school program leaders. Others have used it in their weekday home meetings.

5. Others use it as an option for new believers' classes.

Full STS Live, With No Responses:

1. If a group is very large, or not in an environment where people can give you responses, you will have to alter your STS style. This can be done. All parts of the STS process (except asking the story to be retold) can be done by one person without expecting an audible response from the people you are teaching. Ask rhetorical questions and just make sure to give time for people to think of their answers.

2. STS stories can be presented on the radio or TV. The retelling is left out, but the other parts of the process remain. The key, especially on radio, is to fill up to five seconds of space after each question with some kind of "meaningless" chatter.

We say "meaningless" because if you are still saying meaningful words, people will be listening to you and will NOT be thinking of their answers to your questions. For example, these are meaningful words: "So what do you think?" "Do you have an idea of what happened next?" "What would you say?" "Your answer is?"

Meaningless chatter is defined as sounds people say that have no meaning, but that fill in spaces of silence. Those meaningless sounds do not distract the listeners by making them listen to you, but they fill the airways so that people will not change the station because they do not hear any sound coming from the radio. For example, meaningless sounds could be "Hmmmmmm?" "Ahhhhhhhhh?" "Un-huh. Un-huh." "Ummmmmmm."

There is a radio sample of Martha-Mary on the STS web site that incorporates that style of meaningless chatter.

3.   If you are skilled at STS and have a way to place 3 or 4 people by microphones in a radio studio, you can produce a fascinating radio program. The first STS storyteller we know that used this format was that storyteller in the Philippines. After a few months of weekly broadcasts, the station was receiving 1,400 participatory texts and phone-ins for each program! Other radio formats have been used very successfully.

Dramas, Fun and Powerful.

Dramas are fun to present and to watch, and they can make stories more realistic. Use them as another way to do the first telling of the story.

Ask helpers to silently act out the parts of the characters in the story. Helpers may add appropriate sound effects, but **always** the storyteller speaks the words as they act out the story. Because the listeners still hear just one storyteller present the whole story, they will be able to retell the story back to you. Likewise, listeners who hear a whole story told by just one person are able to return home and retell that story to family members and others who did not hear it.

We do not encourage helpers to actually speak the words of the characters. If you let the different helpers speak the lines, it becomes a play. Although presenting a story through a play is entertaining and can enlighten those in attendance, the story loses its ability to be retold.

Also, having many people speaking lines makes accurate presentation of a story difficult, since many people have to learn and remember their spoken parts. During presentation, when lines are forgotten, a serious Bible story can quickly turn into a comedy. Be very careful that the serious message of a story does not become silly.

The God's Story Project Offers Ways to Learn and Ways to Spread STS—as Well as Multiple Resources

1.   **STS Handbook.** This STS handbook, in audio or written format, details the STS process.

2. **STS Vision Casting.** As instructors are available, we offer presentations that can be from two hours up to two days in length. We demonstrate STS, explain the concept and share impact results. If this vision casting is a 4-hour or longer presentation, we provide some hands-on experience.

3. **STS Three-day Workshop.** This model offers demonstration and explanation of STS and hands-on participation by attendees. From these three days of training, many attendees acquire enough skills to be practitioners who, with practice, can minister using stories.

4. **STS One-Stop Workshop.** We feature these two-part overlapping workshops as they provide a forum that, over time, produces qualified STS instructors. These instructors can then, in turn, train others. This workshop is an ideal choice when a team of instructors needs to come from a great distance to train, or when attendees are gathered from many distant places.

   During the first 14 hours, a small group is taught, with one instructor for every three attendees. After the 14 hours of intensive teaching and practice, these newly trained practitioners step into the role of Assistant Instructors. They assist in the training of a larger group of attendees who come for an additional 19 hours of instruction. This additional "workshop" is done with a ratio of one Assistant Instructor for every five attendees.

   After this 33 hours of training, spread over 5 days, most of these Assistant Instructors can become Provisional Instructors, who, with further practice and leadership experience, can become Certified Instructors.

5. **STS Church Multiplier Workshop.** This workshop uses some combination of Friday night, Saturday and Sunday, or just Saturday and Sunday. In four successive weekends of 14 teaching-hours each, all of the members of an average size church can become competent STS practitioners.

   In five to seven weeks, everyone in a larger church (up to 50,000 members) can be trained. As well, a core of the people trained will be able to be certified as STS instructors. Amazingly, in these Multiplier Workshops, most of the people participating only need to attend one or two of the weekend trainings to achieve this total church coverage!

6. **STS Home Workshop**: One certified STS instructor invites three believers to a workshop held in a home. The instructor leads 2 ½ hour

sessions, once-a-week, for six weeks to complete a workshop. Sessions can be held on evenings, afternoons or weekends.

This style of workshop allows participation by those who, because of jobs or family obligations, cannot break away long enough to attend a one-day or longer workshop. In addition, homes offer a comfortable, nonthreatening learning environment for shy folks. We provide needed guidelines, some material and the schedule for training.

After six sessions, this one instructor will have trained those three people to be useful STS practitioners. Those three new practitioners are then encouraged to attend a second 6-week Home Workshop. They are to invite three new people each.

As we do in our Five-Day and Church Multiplier workshops, gradually the instructor guides the newly trained practitioners into leadership. By the end of the second six-week session of training, the original three have helped train three more people each. Additionally, they have added to their STS skill and have experience as Assistant Instructors.

Attendees may continue training others or decide to gather weekly to study God's Word, now as a home Bible study or fellowship group.

If these twelve want to continue the process of inviting three more each and training them, then after the next six-week session, the group will have grown to 36 (plus the original instructor.) Many homes can accommodate this quantity of people. A lot of the STS hands-on training is done in small groups, so these groups of four can scatter in other rooms or sometimes meet outdoors.

The people newly trained in STS might continue to expand their number by training more practitioners. They could start home groups or use their Bible storytelling/teaching skills for evangelism. Or, they may simply use STS-style Bible study to grow closer to the Lord. We see all of these directions as wonderful.

Because STS skills equip people to very effectively learn and share Scripture, their lives, and the lives of those to whom they tell and teach stories, will be impacted for the glory of God.

If a majority of those trained go on to train others, in two years that first Home Workshop led by one Certified Instructor could impact over 6,000 people! This is a natural, workable model of discipleship and mentoring. Since the STS concept centers on listening to God's Word and making personal application, we can see why the impact and multiplication is so great.

7. **Discipleship-Multiplication.** People leave STS workshops as story practitioners, equipped to use their new skills one-on-one or in groups. Various media and curriculum, such as the *Practitioner Guide*, show how to continue building skills while ministering with stories. Most importantly, this information gives guidelines to hand off small amounts of how-to-do STS instruction to those you teach—while ministering! (Top links on web site, "Training Info" and "Resources," lead to the various selections available.)

8. **Brochures.** Tri-folds with descriptions, testimonies and ways to share STS and *God's Story*. Ask about other brochures on specialized topics and places to utilize STS.

9. **Practitioner Audio Training.** In-depth STS Bible-story preparation experience designed for interactive group discussion. Groups spend 2 to 6 hours discussing and discovering! Available on MP3, CD or solar players. Multiple languages.

10. **Interactive Discovery of the Bible.** Bible stories with rhetorical and group questions. Use for schools, classes and home groups. Believers and seekers heartily participate. Average time 60 to 90 minutes, DVD and audio. Multiple languages.

11. **SimplyTheStory.org** offers a wealth of information about STS in written, audio and video. See details on STS, its beginning, FAQs, apologetics, downloadable resources, testimonies of use worldwide, upcoming trainings, Oral Bible Schools, sample stories and more. Use the 3-minute video, *What & Why,* in churches to vision-cast STS training for short-term mission trips. Resources and articles continually being added to the STS website.

12. **Live Practice and Mentoring**. Consider joining live Skype story-practice sessions and mentoring via STS Extension Classes.

13. **Audio Handbook.** Recorded CD of STS Handbook is available. Look for the DVD on STS training.

14. **Twitter.** Follow STS at http://www.twitter.com/SimplyTheStory

15. **Hosting.** If you want to know what it takes to host a workshop, please contact your nearest country director as listed at the end of this handbook. Go to the STS web site and search for "hosting" to obtain all of the guidelines.

Appendix A: Coaching Review Forms

Storyteller _____ Instructor _____ Date _____

Details of *Simply The Story* process are in the STS Handbook. Remind storytellers, "I will coach you afterwards. Before starting your story presentation, remember this. No matter how literate your workshop comrades may be, **you are to present your story as if those in the listening audience are oral communicators** and they only know the content of the story you present (and the content of the other stories that have been told during the current training)."

These are reminders for you, the instructor-coach. Storytellers will …
1) Use no extra-biblical information in the introduction.
2) Only if needed give a short pre-story setup (introduction).
3) Maintain accuracy of the Bible story, with no information left out or added.
4) Stay in one Bible story, not combining information from parallel accounts.
5) Deliver thoughtful, encouraging responses to the listeners who respond as volunteers and answer questions.
6) Show spontaneous flexibility in answering the specific questions of the responders.
7) Give an interesting Lead Through that moves quickly through the story using various styles to involve listeners.
8) Lead to observations in the story through a style of questions to which an oral learner can respond.
9) Share Spiritual Applications by asking questions to which an oral learner can respond.
10) Not preach!
11) Not use the story as a springboard to teach a favorite personal topic. Rather, they trust God's skill in communicating truth through the Scripture, and they will let the story speak its messages.
12) Be able to define and demonstrate the 5 separate components of STS presentation.

Ratings in the instructor grading-grid reflect only that the storyteller demonstrated the 5 components of STS. Any category that was skipped or not clearly presented will have a "NTY" rating (Not there yet). Otherwise it will have a "GI" for Got-it!

Instructor Grading-Grid	Date	Story Title	Reference	Story	Retell	Lead Through	Observations	Applications
Name of Storyteller								

Overall Recommendations

Comments for some categories below may be the instructor's compliments when something is done exceptionally well. Comments may be suggestions about areas that need more practice. Many of categories will have nothing written beside them if that part went normally. The checklist helps instructors remember what to say afterwards so the whole STS presentation can be done at once with no interference. Stories can be started again if storyteller gets lost.

Coaching Review for 3 Times of Story Presentation

Story, Comments
1. Introduction
2. Accuracy
3. Listening Interest
4. Stayed in Story
5. Felt Story
6. Actions

Volunteer, Comments
1. Prompting Volunteer
2. Encouraging
3. Correction of Volunteer

Lead Through, Comments
1. Promptly Completed
2. Varied Styles (3)
3. Participation
4. Accuracy

Coaching Review for 2 Kinds of Spiritual Treasures

Spiritual Observations, Comments

1. Use of Key Words
2. Oral Style Questions
3. Gestures As Keys
4. Valid Observations
5. Cross Ways Discussion
6. Group Interaction
7. Kind Interchanges
8. Affirmations
9. Answers In Story
10. Led to Treasures
11. Listened Well
12. Let Story Teach

Spiritual Applications, Comments

1. Oral Style Questions
2. Gestures As Keys
3. Valid Applications
4. Cross Ways Discussion
5. Group Interaction
6. Kind Interchanges
7. Affirmations
8. Applications are in Story
9. Led or Told Applications
10. Answers Attainable
11. Avoided Preaching

Overall Handling of Group

1. Problem Management
2. Response to Any Out-of- Story Questions
3. Group Description

Appendix B: Journey Through a Sample Story
How to Prepare Questions
Zacchaeus, Luke 19:1-10

As this chapter title indicates, we are now going to journey through another sample story. We selected the story of Zacchaeus. This story was selected, partially because Zacchaeus is often seen as a simple story for children. It is—but it is also deep.

The story is often told like this: "A little man named Zacchaeus wanted to see Jesus, so he climbed a tree so he could see over the crowd. The crowd in the story doesn't like this man because he is a tax collector, but Jesus notices the little man and comes to the man's home for lunch. Zacchaeus is happy and gives half of his money to the poor people, and we should be like Zacchaeus."

Although the information just mentioned is inside this story—there is much, much more to be found. As we go through the story STS style, many of the story's deep treasures will be uncovered.

As we explore the Zacchaeus story, we will be using a different style to communicate the process of STS, and we will be concentrating on just one part of STS—the forming of questions.

There will be a written form of questions that represents what is usually done in your thoughts. Since we are not with you in person, to talk about preparation, we chose the second best method of transferring the mental process to you— we wrote it.

This preparation of a Bible story is a specific progression of finding treasures and forming questions from those treasures. When you do this in your mind, the story becomes your notes. The story is like a clothesline. As you slowly walk alongside the clothesline in your mind, you hang your treasures and questions on your line.

When you see the size of this sample journey, you may exclaim in shock, "This is too long!" Then, as you start through it, you could say (as have others), "There is too much repetition!" Honestly, the sample may not fit your learning style. We do encourage you to at least try learning from it to see if it will help you in the forming of questions.

Actually, for some people, this chapter is where they gained clarity about how to form questions.

At first, when you explore the *Zacchaeus* story on your own, you probably will not find as many treasures as we present here. Note that we have taught this story in many places around the world and, during those times, have learned much from this story through discussing it with others. This information we have accumulated over time, enables us now to share a lot of those treasures with you. In actuality, you will be gleaning information from many others, which is what happens in STS through group contribution.

As you continue to prepare and present stories STS style, you too will discover more and more treasures. In fact, you may even go back to this story later and find additional treasures! God's Word is like that. You will never exhaust its supply of truths!

This chapter is designed as follows: After you read and learn the *Zacchaeus* story, we show you how to hunt for the spiritual treasures in the story and then form questions to help lead others to those treasures.

You may not see, or even agree with, some of the Spiritual Observations that we suggest. That is not uncommon. It should not be considered a problem. When you use the STS style to teach others, you would share only what you personally, clearly see within a story.

Some ideas we offer may just be that—ideas to discuss. As the ideas are discussed in a group, very often the Lord speaks through others, and a new understanding within that Scripture passage will come to light.

We know that developing the questions to lead others to discovery is one of the most challenging parts of STS. We hope the repetition here will help you become more comfortable with this new skill.

When you actually teach this story, because of shortness of time or other reasons, you may only present a few of these treasures at any one time.

Now Let's Get Started

It is recommended for this exercise that you first learn this ten-verse story in STS style. (The text of the story is found below.)

Learn the story as described earlier in the section, How to Prepare a Story:

1.   Read this ten-verse story one time through, **out loud**.

2.   As you read it, speak it in your naturally spoken words. For instance, instead of saying "publican" you might say "tax collector."

3.   See in your mind's eye what is happening in the story.

4. Immediately after you complete your reading, close your eyes and repeat as much as you remember in the story out loud. You are trying to remember the exact story, not the exact words.

5. Go back and read it out loud again. You will notice the parts you left out.

6. Close your eyes and again repeat the story **out loud**.

Often, after about four times of reading and repeating the story this way, people will notice that they are able to tell the whole story fairly accurately!

If, however, after four to six times through, people are still struggling with remembering the content of the story, there is a strong possibility that they have inadvertently slipped back into a familiar style of memorizing words, rather than the new way of remembering content.

They have changed the STS recipe!

If you are struggling with being able to remember the story, we encourage you to go back and review and follow the steps above and try learning this *Zacchaeus* story again, STS style. This time, no sneaking a peak at the written story when you are trying to repeat the story. And remember, read **out loud** and repeat **out loud!**

> And Jesus entered and passed through Jericho. And, look, there was a man named Zacchaeus, who was the chief tax collector, and he was rich. And Zacchaeus tried to see who Jesus was; but couldn't because of the large crowd, because Zacchaeus was short in height. So Zacchaeus ran ahead, and climbed up into a sycamore tree to see Jesus: because Jesus was going to pass by that way.
>
> And when Jesus came to that place, he looked up, and saw Zacchaeus, and said unto him, "Zacchaeus, hurry, and come down; for today I must stay at your house." And Zacchaeus hurried, and came down, and joyfully received Jesus. And when the crowd saw it, they all murmured, saying that Jesus was gone to be a guest with a man that is a sinner.
>
> And Zacchaeus stood, and said to the Lord, "Look, Lord, half of my possessions I give to the poor; and if I have taken anything from any man by false accusation, I restore to him four times as much." And Jesus said to Zacchaeus, "This day salvation is come to this house, seeing that Zacchaeus also is a son of Abraham. For the Son of Man is come to seek and to save that which was lost." (Luke 19:1-10)

Please Take Careful Notice

After preparing your story, you may find that you are not able to substantiate the validity of all of the thoughts you had while preparing your story. When it comes time to teach, those unsubstantiated thoughts should not be used to teach others. Just set those ideas aside, perhaps to be used another time when you prepare a different story. You will find that sometimes as you present your story and are asking questions, the Lord will speak some added truth to you through the responses of others. At that time, your earlier thoughts may be verified as true!

Before reading any further, we suggest that you spend some time thinking through the *Zacchaeus* story to see what spiritual treasures you can discover. This exercise will give you an opportunity to practice your skills and then, with the story fresh in your mind, you can compare your observations to ours. You may find some treasures that we don't mention. Likewise, we may have found some that you hadn't noticed. Enjoy your treasure hunt!

Some of the Spiritual Observations We See:

1. People who seemed to be interested in Jesus blocked Zacchaeus from getting close to Jesus.

2. This man Zacchaeus was small in height, but big in position. He was a rich man and head tax collector, but he was so intent on seeing Jesus, that when the easy approach didn't work, he purposely chose to go out of his way.

3. The probability that people might ridicule this man of importance for his undignified act of running down the street in public and climbing the tree didn't stop Zacchaeus from doing those things.

4. We saw Jesus walking down the street in the middle of a crush of people crowding around Him. Although all the people were pushing in against Jesus, He bypassed all of them and chose to notice just one person who was not even nearby, and this man was in a tree!

5. Jesus called Zacchaeus by name, which shows His personal interest in the man.

6. Jesus invited Himself to Zacchaeus' home, which is kind of presumptuous in most cultures. It shows Jesus' knowledge and confidence of what "must" take place.

7. When a person looks up, especially a leader who people are following, the people would also turn their eyes up to see what the leader is looking at. That would mean that it was not just Jesus seeing Zacchaeus, it was all the people! Zacchaeus didn't show fear or embarrassment at being "discovered." In fact, he showed joy.

8. Zacchaeus didn't hesitate to respond precisely to Jesus' summons. He hurried.

9. The crowd spoke against Zacchaeus by murmuring among themselves about Jesus, how He had "gone to be a guest with a man that is a sinner." "Gone…with" can indicate that Jesus was just leaving or that He had left.

    Exactly when Zacchaeus and Jesus knew of the crowd's criticism of Jesus' decision to go to Zacchaeus' house is unclear. But later in the story, by what Jesus said to the crowd in front of Zacchaeus, we see that both Zacchaeus and Jesus did know of their criticism. But Zacchaeus did not let himself be influenced by the crowd's criticism. He still welcomed Jesus into his home.

10. The crowd's criticism saying that Jesus has "gone to be a guest with a man that is a sinner," implies that the crowd thought that they were NOT sinners.

11. The crowd acted as if they were "followers" of Jesus. They moved along, pressing against Jesus. Although their criticism implied that they cared about who Jesus ate with, it seems like they were insinuating that one of their homes would have been the right selection. Actually, the crowd was showing total disrespect for Jesus by disagreeing with Him on His choice of homes to visit.

12. This judgmental crowd had its beliefs, but did not seem to have the nerve to question Jesus to His face. The crowd had no idea of Jesus' power, behaving as if He could not hear their complaints if they just talked among themselves.

13. Zacchaeus, a wealthy man, demonstrated his heart when he referred to giving half of his goods to the poor.

14. Zacchaeus announced that if he had lied to take anything from anyone, he wanted to restore to that person four times what he had taken. Zacchaeus did not say "if" he was indicted or found guilty by the law that he would return four times the stolen amount. Zacchaeus pledged to do this of his own free will. Some might suggest that

Zacchaeus had already been giving his money to the poor, but the opinion of the crowd shows us differently.

If he was a tax collector who gave half of his money to the poor, possibly he already could have been doing that secretly. But to have already restored four times to all who he may have defrauded would have put Zacchaeus in the class of a righteous person in the eyes of the crowd.

What we do know from the story is that, at some point in the episode, Zacchaeus admitted that he was a sinner and wanted to make things right. Jesus said that salvation happened that day. We do see that Zacchaeus showed incredible generosity.

15. At first it could be thought that Zacchaeus might have been trying to purchase spiritual acceptance from Jesus. But we know Zacchaeus came to faith in Jesus that day because Jesus said to him, "This day is salvation come to this house." Zacchaeus is the only person in the story who admitted he was a sinner and the only one in the story who gained salvation.

16. In the story, Jesus said directly to Zacchaeus, "This day is salvation come to this house." Jesus continued speaking and said, "seeing that Zacchaeus also is a son of Abraham." From this we see that others besides Zacchaeus were present. Also, by what Jesus said, we see that He changed who He was speaking to and Jesus was defending Zacchaeus to these people!

17. Jesus' statement, that the purpose of His coming "is to seek and to save that which is lost," definitely honored Zacchaeus and seems to be a summary statement that criticized the crowd.

18. At first, it is obvious that Zacchaeus was seeking Jesus. Then part way through the story, it becomes a story of Jesus seeking out Zacchaeus!

Forming Observation Questions:

Now, for practice, we will show you how to form questions that can lead others to each of the observations listed above. You will see that sometimes we may use several questions to draw the listeners to an observation.

Since each question is formed to lead listeners to the Spiritual Observations, as a help we relist the observations listed as "SO." The question or questions that will lead to that observation are written as

"SOQ." This will help you better understand how to gradually lead others to discover the observation. It's like leading a bird to a cage by laying down a trail of little bread crumbs.

1. **SO** – People who seemed to be interested in Jesus blocked Zacchaeus from getting close to Jesus.

    SOQ –
    - In this story we saw that Zacchaeus wanted to see Jesus, but he couldn't get close to Jesus. Besides the fact that Zacchaeus was short, we saw in the story that people got in Zacchaeus' way. What were the people doing that caused them to block Zacchaeus?
    - So are you saying that the people who wanted to be close to Jesus prevented a seeker from seeing Jesus?
    - What do you think about that?

2. **SO** – This man Zacchaeus was small in height, but big in position. He was a rich man and head tax collector, but he was so intent on seeing Jesus, that when the easy approach didn't work, he purposely chose to go out of his way.

    SOQ –
    - How would you describe Zacchaeus' social, business and economic status in the community?
    - So, Zacchaeus used a bit of his wealth and hired some big ruffians to break a path through the crowd, right? No?
    - Okay, then what do we see here? When this man of importance wasn't able to see Jesus using the normal or easy method, to what extremes did Zacchaeus go?

3. **SO** – The probability that people might ridicule this man of importance for his undignified act of running down the street in public and climbing the tree didn't stop Zacchaeus from doing those things.

    SOQ –
    - Did we see in the story what the people of the area thought of Zacchaeus?
    - Zacchaeus was a man of importance and he knows that people consider him an unworthy individual. Does this seem normal to you? Might there be any personal risk to Zacchaeus to be seen running down the road in public and climbing up a tree to see Jesus? How so?

4. **SO** – We saw Jesus walking down the street in the middle of a crush of people crowding around Him. Although all the people were

pushing in against Jesus, He bypassed all of them and chose to notice just one person who was not even nearby, and this man was in a tree!

SOQ –
- When Jesus was walking down a street surrounded by a crowd, which of the people in the crowd did He respond to?
- What might Jesus' behavior show us?

5. **SO** – Jesus called Zacchaeus by name which shows His personal interest in the man.

    SOQ – I wonder, is there anything in what Jesus said to Zacchaeus that shows personal interest?

6. **SO** – Jesus invited Himself to Zacchaeus' home which is kind of presumptuous in most cultures. It shows Jesus' knowledge and confidence of what "must" take place.

    SOQ – Who do you see taking the lead in the conversation and how was this invitation kind of unusual?

7. **SO** – When a person looks up, especially a leader who people are following, the people would also turn their eyes up to see what the leader is looking at. That would mean that it was not just Jesus seeing Zacchaeus, it was all the people! Zacchaeus didn't show fear or embarrassment at being "discovered." In fact, he showed joy.

    SOQ –
    - Have you ever been in a group of people and one of them looked upward and stared at something?
    - What did the rest of the people in the group do?
    - Do we know from the story if anyone else besides Jesus saw Zacchaeus in the tree? How?
    - So this man Zacchaeus was caught in a very embarrassing situation and everyone SAW him! How might a rich and powerful person feel at the moment of being discovered in a silly kind of a place, such as up a tree?
    - Did Zacchaeus try to hide or make excuses?
    - I wonder, Can we know from the story how Zacchaeus felt?

8. **SO** – Zacchaeus didn't hesitate to respond precisely to Jesus' summons. He hurried.

    SOQ – So, how did Zacchaeus respond when Jesus called him down? Exactly how?

9. **SO** – The crowd spoke against Zacchaeus by murmuring among themselves about Jesus, how He had "gone to be a guest with a man that is a sinner." "Gone...with" can indicate that Jesus was just leaving or that He had left.

Exactly when Zacchaeus and Jesus knew of the crowd's criticism of Jesus' decision to go to Zacchaeus' house is unclear. But later in the story, by what Jesus said to the crowd in front of Zacchaeus, we see that both Zacchaeus and Jesus did know of their criticism. But Zacchaeus did not let himself be influenced by the crowd's criticism. He still welcomed Jesus into his home.

SOQ –
- We know that the crowd felt superior to Zacchaeus by what they murmured. Does Zacchaeus seem to be influenced by the crowd?
- How did he react to their criticism?
- How else could Zacchaeus have responded to the crowd's criticism?
- What kinds of things might we learn about Zacchaeus from his nonresponse to the crowd?

10. **SO** – The crowd's criticism saying that Jesus has "gone to be a guest with a man that is a sinner," implies that the crowd thought that they were NOT sinners.

SOQ –
- Could what the people in the crowd said to each other maybe show us anything about Zacchaeus—spiritually?
- Based on what the crowd said, could we get any idea of what the crowd thought of themselves—spiritually?

11. **SO** – The crowd acted as if they were "followers" of Jesus. They moved along, pressing against Jesus. Although their criticism implied that they cared about who Jesus ate with, it seems like they were insinuating that one of their homes would have been the right selection. Actually, the crowd was showing total disrespect for Jesus by disagreeing with Him on His choice of homes to visit.

SOQ –
- I wonder, in the beginning of the story, is there anything that could make us think of the crowd as "followers" of Jesus?
- The crowd moved along pressing against Jesus. By their physical actions and by their apparent interest in who Jesus spent His personal time with, what might they be indicating?

- But when it comes down to it, what respect do they seem to be showing Jesus?

12. **SO** – This judgmental crowd had its beliefs, but did not seem to have the nerve to question Jesus to His face. The crowd had no idea of Jesus' power, behaving as if He could not hear their complaints if they just talked among themselves.

SOQ –
- Do you remember how the crowd was confused so they asked Jesus how it was that He would leave everyone who wanted to be with Him and go to the home of a sinner? No? They didn't. What did they do?
- So what in their behavior might show us whether or not they truly respected Jesus?

13. **SO** – Zacchaeus, a wealthy man, demonstrated his heart when he referred to giving half of his goods to the poor.

SOQ –
- What generous pledge did Zacchaeus make?
- Could that show us anything about his values?

14. **SO** – Zacchaeus announced that if he had lied to take anything from anyone, he wanted to restore to that person four times what he had taken. Zacchaeus did not say "if" he was indicted or found guilty by the law that he would return four times the stolen amount. Zacchaeus pledged to do this of his own free will. Some might suggest that Zacchaeus had already been giving his money to the poor, but the opinion of the crowd shows us differently.

If he was a tax collector who gave half of his money to the poor, possibly he already could have been doing that secretly. But to have already restored four times to all who he may have defrauded would have put Zacchaeus in the class of a righteous person in the eyes of the crowd.

What we do know from the story is that, at some point in the episode, Zacchaeus admitted that he was a sinner and wanted to make things right. Jesus said that salvation happened that day. We do see that Zacchaeus showed incredible generosity.

SOQ –
- Is there anything in the story that might indicate that Zacchaeus had been discovered by the law to be a thief, or

that he was indicted or found guilty by the law, so now he is trying to pay his way out of trouble?

- Can we know from the story whether Zacchaeus had already been returning money before meeting Jesus, or, do you think he may have decided to do that when Jesus visited?
- Can we tell by the crowd's opinion of Zacchaeus if he had been an incredibly honest tax collector and had already been sharing half of his money with the poor?
- How difficult do you think it might be for Zacchaeus to personally go back to those he had falsely accused and had taken money from—and to return that money?
- Can we see from the story whether or not this encounter with Jesus changed Zacchaeus' life? How do you see that?

15. **SO** – At first it could be thought that Zacchaeus might have been trying to purchase spiritual acceptance from Jesus. But we know Zacchaeus came to faith in Jesus that day because Jesus said to him, "This day is salvation come to this house." Zacchaeus is the only person in the story who admitted he was a sinner and the only one in the story who gained salvation.

SOQ –
- How many people in the story seem to show an interest in Jesus?
- Do you think in this story that Zacchaeus was trying to buy favor with Jesus?
- Is there anything in the story that would help us to know whether or not Zacchaeus really had a genuine spiritual change in his life that day?
- Could what Jesus said about Zacchaeus show that Zacchaeus did come to faith?
- Who in this story admitted to being a sinner?
- Who in the story did not see themselves as sinners?
- Out of all those in the story, who gained salvation?
- From this story, what might be found about the difference between those who have access to Jesus and come to faith and those who have access, but do not come to faith?

16. **SO** – In the story, Jesus said directly to Zacchaeus, "This day is salvation come to this house." Jesus continued speaking and said, "seeing that Zacchaeus also is a son of Abraham." From this we see that others besides Zacchaeus were present. Also, by what Jesus said, we see that He changed who He was speaking to and that Jesus was defending Zacchaeus to these people!

SOQ –

- In this story, as Zacchaeus was making his confession of faith to Jesus, it seemed like it was just the two of them having this conversation. But when Jesus said, "seeing as he also is a son of Abraham," do you see any indication that others may have been present?
- I mean, at first Jesus was talking to Zacchaeus and then He is saying "he." So, who does Jesus seem to be speaking to?
- Does Jesus seem to be defending Zacchaeus in some way?
- What might Jesus be trying to get these people to see about themselves and about Zacchaeus?

17. **SO** – Jesus' statement, that the purpose of His coming "is to seek and to save that which is lost," definitely honored Zacchaeus and seems to be a summary statement that criticized the crowd.

SOQ –

- Jesus ended this story by saying that the purpose of His coming was to "seek and to save that which was lost." What do you see in Jesus' summary statement?
- Do you think Jesus was trying to get the crowd to see things about themselves?
- Explain your ideas.

18. **SO** – At first, it is obvious that Zacchaeus was seeking Jesus. Then part way through the story, it becomes a story of Jesus seeking out Zacchaeus!

SOQ –

- So far in this story, would you say that Zacchaeus is seeking Jesus?
- What might show us this?
- But as we look again at the story, would you say that Jesus is seeking Zacchaeus?
- Where do you see that in the story?
- So which is it? Is Zacchaeus seeking Jesus or is Jesus seeking Zacchaeus?
- Can both be true? What do you think?

Spiritual Applications We See:

The next step is to prepare Spiritual Applications. To help you see how **each application needs to be based on a specific observation** we will once again relist our observations. Each observation will be followed by its related Spiritual Application.

Finally, as was done for the questions leading to the observations, we will help you learn how to form questions to lead to the Spiritual Applications. In this section you will find each Spiritual Observation followed by its related Spiritual Application and then the questions that lead to that application.

We have included all this repetition so you can review the way questions lead listeners to observations, observations lead to applications, and then questions lead listeners to those applications. We also know that developing the questions to lead others to discovery is one of the most challenging parts of STS.

Following is a list of Spiritual Applications. Each one is based on the Spiritual Observations above. For ease in following the process, the Spiritual Observations are included, again designated as "SO," and immediately after each SO the Spiritual Application is listed as "SA."

1. **SO** – People who seemed to be interested in Jesus blocked Zacchaeus from getting close to Jesus.

    SA – We who claim to follow Jesus can sometimes be so focused on getting close to Jesus (or being religious) that we unwittingly or carelessly keep people away who are seeking Jesus.

2. **SO** – This man Zacchaeus was small in height, but big in position. He was a rich man and head tax collector, but he was so intent on seeing Jesus, that when the easy approach didn't work, he purposely chose to go out of his way.

    SA – When we want to seek Jesus, we must be ready to set aside our pride and do what is needed to seek Him and to follow Him.

3. **SO** – The probability that people might ridicule this man of importance for his undignified act of running down the street in public and climbing the tree didn't stop Zacchaeus from doing those things.

    SA – We must never let pride, or the fear of what people might say about us, keep us from getting to know Jesus. Even if what we have to do might be looked at by others as foolish or beneath our social position, we must do it anyway.

4. **SO** – We saw Jesus walking down the street in the middle of a crush of people crowding around Him. Although all the people were pushing in against Jesus, He bypassed all of them and chose to notice just one person who was not even nearby, and this man was in a tree!

5. **SA** – Many people that day sought favor with God. They appeared to be interested in Jesus, but Jesus ignored them and selected only one person. Many people in the world act as if they are interested in God, but, like the people in the story, many of them are not genuine. Jesus called out to one who was genuine. God knows our hearts and knows if we are truly seeking Him.

6. **SO** – Jesus called Zacchaeus by name, which shows His personal interest in the man.

   SA – We see here a personal God, one who knows where we are and knows us by name. If we understand that God is merciful to those who seek Him, we want Him to know us by name—to be known by Him personally is comforting. Zacchaeus had been eager to see Jesus, so when Jesus called him by name, Zacchaeus responded with joy.

7. **SO** – Jesus invited Himself to Zacchaeus' home, which is kind of presumptuous in most cultures. It shows Jesus' knowledge and confidence of what "must" take place.

   SA – It is amazing and encouraging that Jesus wants to be with those who seek Him.

8. **SO** – When a person looks up, especially a leader who people are following, the people would also turn their eyes up to see what the leader is looking at. That would mean that it was not just Jesus seeing Zacchaeus, it was all the people! Zacchaeus didn't show fear or embarrassment at being "discovered." In fact, he showed joy.

   SA – When we are looked at by unbelievers and unfaithful followers of God and thought to be silly or not intelligent for wanting to know God, we must not let them influence us. When we know that God is interested in us personally, we should react with joy.

8. **SO** – Zacchaeus didn't hesitate to respond precisely to Jesus' summons. He hurried.

   SA – If at any time we know God is calling us to action, we must respond—and respond according to His instructions. Delayed obedience could be the same as disobedience.

9. **SO** – The crowd spoke against Zacchaeus by murmuring among themselves about Jesus, how He had "gone to be a guest with a man that is a sinner." "Gone...with" can indicate that Jesus was just leaving or that He had left.

Exactly when Zacchaeus and Jesus knew of the crowd's criticism of Jesus' decision to go to Zacchaeus' house is unclear. But later in the story, by what Jesus said to the crowd in front of Zacchaeus, we see that both Zacchaeus and Jesus did know of their criticism. But Zacchaeus did not let himself be influenced by the crowd's criticism. He still welcomed Jesus into his home.

SA – We can start out well. But we must stay the course, even if we receive criticism from those around us—even from a religious crowd.

10. **SO** – The crowd's criticism saying that Jesus has "gone to be a guest with a man that is a sinner," implies that the crowd thought that they were NOT sinners.

    SA – Out of their own mouths, proud people condemn themselves. Let us not be like those proud people who will not admit that they have sin.

11. **SO** – The crowd acted as if they were "followers" of Jesus. They moved along, pressing against Jesus. Although their criticism implied that they cared about who Jesus ate with, it seems like they were insinuating that one of their homes would have been the right selection. Actually, the crowd was showing total disrespect for Jesus by disagreeing with Him on His choice of homes to visit.

    SA – Not all who claim to be followers of Jesus really know Him nor do they actually respect Him or His decisions. Not all religious people show respect for God's Word.

12. **SO** – This judgmental crowd had its beliefs, but did not seem to have the nerve to question Jesus to His face. The crowd had no idea of Jesus' power, behaving as if He could not hear their complaints if they just talked among themselves.

    SA – The crowd's actions were much like people today who think God cannot hear what they whisper to each other or see what they do in the dark and hidden places.

13. **SO** – Zacchaeus, a wealthy man, demonstrated his heart when he referred to giving half of his goods to the poor.

    SA – A true encounter with Jesus will produce a change in one's worldview and values.

14. **SO** – Zacchaeus announced that if he had lied to take anything from anyone, he wanted to restore to that person four times what he had

taken. Zacchaeus did not say "if" he was indicted or found guilty by the law that he would return four times the stolen amount. Zacchaeus pledged to do this of his own free will. Some might suggest that Zacchaeus had already been giving his money to the poor, but the opinion of the crowd shows us differently.

If he was a tax collector who gave half of his money to the poor, possibly he already could have been doing that secretly. But to have already restored four times to all who he may have defrauded would have put Zacchaeus in the class of a righteous person in the eyes of the crowd.

What we do know from the story is that, at some point in the episode, Zacchaeus admitted that he was a sinner and wanted to make things right. Jesus said that salvation happened that day. We do see that Zacchaeus showed incredible generosity.

SA – Zacchaeus was a wealthy man, a chief tax collector whose greedy ways changed. He became honest and generous. This head tax collector even humbled himself by saying he would admit to those he had wronged that he had lied to them and that he would restore to them four times the amount of money he had stolen. When we come to faith in Jesus and admit our sinfulness, we should show humility and a willingness to go back and generously correct past wrongs.

15. **SO** – At first it could be thought that Zacchaeus might have been trying to purchase spiritual acceptance from Jesus. But we know Zacchaeus came to faith in Jesus that day because Jesus said to him, "This day is salvation come to this house." Zacchaeus is the only person in the story who admitted he was a sinner and the only one in the story who gained salvation.

    SA – Salvation cannot come to those who do not first admit to being sinners.

16. **SO** – In the story, Jesus said directly to Zacchaeus, "This day is salvation come to this house." Jesus continued speaking and said, "seeing that Zacchaeus also is a son of Abraham." From this we see that others besides Zacchaeus were present. Also, by what Jesus said, we see that He changed who He was speaking to and Jesus was defending Zacchaeus to these people!

    SA – We saw Jesus working with Zacchaeus and Zacchaeus turning in faith to Jesus. But all the while, that critical crowd was there watching. Jesus was still reaching out to this self-righteous crowd, trying to get them to see themselves as needy and to open their minds to see that Zacchaeus was worthy of God's attention. Today there is still a self-righteous crowd that criticizes people whose lives change when they follow Jesus.

17. **SO** – Jesus' statement, that the purpose of His coming "is to seek and to save that which is lost," definitely honored Zacchaeus and seems to be a summary statement that criticized the crowd.

    SA – If we want approval by God, we need to admit our lostness and sinfulness and allow God to save us.

18. **SO** – At first, it is obvious that Zacchaeus was seeking Jesus. Then part way through the story, it becomes a story of Jesus seeking out Zacchaeus!

    SA – We saw in the story that Zacchaeus did seek Jesus, but also Jesus did seek Zacchaeus. Both are true. We must seek God. But know, at the same time, He seeks us!

Forming Spiritual Application Questions:

Now lastly, move on and look next at the questions we formed that will lead to Spiritual Applications. The Spiritual Observations and the Spiritual Applications are listed again so you can see the full sequence. Note especially the Spiritual Applications on which the questions are based. Those Spiritual Application questions are written below after the abbreviation of "SAQ."

1. **SO** – People who seemed to be interested in Jesus blocked Zacchaeus from getting close to Jesus.

    SA – We who claim to follow Jesus can sometimes be so focused on getting close to Jesus (or being religious) that we unwittingly or carelessly keep people away who are seeking Jesus.

    SAQ –
    - Is it possible today for people who act religious to stand in the way of a sincere seeker of God?
    - In what way could that happen?

2. **SO** – This man Zacchaeus was small in height, but big in position. He was a rich man and head tax collector, but he was so intent on seeing Jesus, that when the easy approach didn't work, he purposely chose to go out of his way.

SA – When we want to seek Jesus, we must be ready to set aside our pride and do what is needed to seek Him and to follow Him.

SAQ –
- Like Zacchaeus, might there be times today that people would have to set aside pride to come close to Jesus?
- When might that time be?
- Can anyone share a time when you or someone you know experienced this?

3. **SO** – The probability that people might ridicule this man of importance for his undignified act of running down the street in public and climbing the tree didn't stop Zacchaeus from doing those things.

    SA – We must never let pride, or the fear of what people might say about us, keep us from getting to know Jesus. Even if what we have to do might be looked at by others as foolish or beneath our social position, we must do it anyway.

    SAQ –
    - Might there be times today when people ridicule those who are seeking God?
    - How does it feel to be ridiculed?
    - Have you, or someone you know personally, ever been mocked for following the Lord? Or have you ever had to do something humiliating to find out more about the Lord?
    - Would it be tempting for us to avoid ridicule if we could?
    - What example in this story of Zacchaeus might help us make the right decision?

4. **SO** – We saw Jesus walking down the street in the middle of a crush of people crowding around Him. Although all the people were pushing in against Jesus, He bypassed all of them and chose to notice just one person who was not even nearby, and this man was in a tree!

    SA – Many people that day sought favor with God. They appeared to be interested in Jesus, but Jesus ignored them and selected only one person. Many people in the world act as if they are interested in God, but many of them are not genuine. Jesus called out to one who was genuine. God knows our hearts and knows if we are truly seeking Him.

    SAQ –
    - What percentage of people in the world do you think are part of some religion?

- Have you ever met religious people who are not truly followers of God?
- With that in mind, and considering those we saw in this story, let's look at this. Of the religious people in the world, do you think there are some who just follow their religion and some who are true seekers of God?
- What happened in this story that identified the true seeker?

5. **SO** – Jesus calls Zacchaeus by name, which shows His personal interest in the man.

SA – We see here a personal God, one who knows where we are and knows us by name. If we understand that God is merciful to those who seek Him, we want Him to know us by name—to be known by Him personally is comforting. Zacchaeus had been eager to see Jesus, so when Jesus called him by name, Zacchaeus responded with joy.

SAQ –
- Does anything about the way Jesus spoke to Zacchaeus bring hope to you?
- Can you explain why?
- Which seems the best: having a God who is impersonal or one who knows you?
- What do you think is good and bad about having a God who knows you?
- Has God ever spoken to you personally?

6. **SO** – Jesus invited Himself to Zacchaeus' home, which is kind of presumptuous in most cultures. It shows Jesus' knowledge and confidence of what "must" take place.

SA – It is amazing and encouraging that Jesus wants to be with those who seek Him.

SAQ –
- What was surprising about the invitation to Zacchaeus' home?
- Was there anything in what Jesus said that showed that the visit definitely would take place?
- What is in the story about Jesus inviting Himself to Zacchaeus' home that might encourage us today to seek God?

7. **SO** – When a person looks up, especially a leader who people are following, the people would also turn their eyes up to see what the leader is looking at. That would mean that it was not just Jesus

seeing Zacchaeus, it was all the people! Zacchaeus didn't show fear or embarrassment at being "discovered." In fact, he showed joy.

SA – When we are looked at by unbelievers and unfaithful followers of God and thought to be silly or not intelligent for wanting to know God, we must not let them influence us. When we know that God is interested in us personally, we should react with joy.

SAQ –
- In a pursuit to know God, does it ever happen that people have to be different than all of the rest of the people in their family or social group or culture?
- Have you ever seen that?
- What do you see in Zacchaeus' behavior and the results of his choices that could encourage us today if we need to be different from someone or something important to us?
- How could what you saw encourage us in our choices today?

8. **SO** – Zacchaeus didn't hesitate to respond precisely to Jesus' summons. He hurried.

SA – If at any time we know God is calling us to action, we must respond—and respond according to His instructions. Delayed obedience could be the same as disobedience.

SAQ –
- Does God call people today?
- If so, in what way might that call come?
- If at any time we know God is calling us to action, how could this story assist us?
- Besides responding quickly, what might God's instructions mean to us? How would you classify "delayed obedience?"

9. **SO** – The crowd spoke against Zacchaeus by murmuring among themselves about Jesus, how He had "gone to be a guest with a man that is a sinner." "Gone...with" can indicate that Jesus was just leaving or that He had left.

Exactly when Zacchaeus and Jesus knew of the crowd's criticism of Jesus' decision to go to Zacchaeus' house is unclear. But later in the story, by what Jesus said to the crowd in front of Zacchaeus, we see that both Zacchaeus and Jesus did know of their criticism. But Zacchaeus did not let himself be influenced by the crowd's criticism. He still welcomed Jesus into his home.

SA – We can start out well. But we must stay the course, even if we receive criticism from those around us—even from a religious crowd.

SAQ –
- The crowd was gossiping openly about Jesus and criticized Zacchaeus. Have you ever been looked at by others who felt superior to you and they openly called you names?
- What did that feel like?
- What could we glean from this story about how to respond to disapproval?

10. **SO** – The crowd's criticism saying that Jesus has "gone to be a guest with a man that is a sinner," implies that the crowd thought that they were NOT sinners.

     SA – Out of their own mouths, proud people condemn themselves. Let us not be like those proud people who will not admit that they have sin.

     SAQ –
     - In your search for God, have you ever had conversations with religious people who thought they were perfect and sinless?
     - How would you describe self-righteousness?
     - Do you think this self-righteousness is something a true follower of God would have—or should have?

11. **SO** – The crowd acted as if they were "followers" of Jesus. They moved along, pressing against Jesus. Although their criticism implied that they cared about who Jesus ate with, it seems like they were insinuating that one of their homes would have been the right selection. Actually, the crowd was showing total disrespect for Jesus by disagreeing with Him on His choice of homes to visit.

     SA – Not all who claim to be followers of Jesus really know Him nor do they actually respect Him or His decisions. Not all religious people show respect for God's Word.

     SAQ –
     - Do you remember how we saw that the crowd acted like they respected Jesus, but showed their true heart by criticizing Jesus' decision on who was invited to be with Jesus?
     - Today, do people ever act like they are followers of God, but really they are more respectful of themselves than of God?
     - What might that look like?

12. **SO** – This judgmental crowd had its beliefs, but did not seem to have the nerve to question Jesus to His face. The crowd had no idea of Jesus' power, behaving as if He could not hear their complaints if they just talked among themselves.

SA – The crowd's actions are much like people today who think God cannot hear what they whisper to each other or see what they do in the dark and hidden places.

SAQ –
   - Do people ever say things in secret or commit acts in the dark, thinking that no one knows what they are doing?
   - What in this story shows us that God knows all we do and say?
   - How should that knowledge affect us?

13. **SO** – Zacchaeus, a wealthy man, demonstrated his heart when he referred to giving half of his goods to the poor.

SA – A true encounter with Jesus will produce a change in one's worldview and values.

SAQ –
   - How might a true encounter with Jesus affect a person's worldview and values?
   - Give some examples.

14. **SO** – Zacchaeus announced that if he had lied to take anything from anyone, he wanted to restore to that person four times what he had taken. Zacchaeus did not say "if" he was indicted or found guilty by the law that he would return four times the stolen amount. Zacchaeus pledged to do this of his own free will. Some might suggest that Zacchaeus had already been giving his money to the poor, but the opinion of the crowd shows us differently.

If he was a tax collector who gave half of his money to the poor, possibly he already could have been doing that secretly. But to have already restored four times to all who he may have defrauded would have put Zacchaeus in the class of a righteous person in the eyes of the crowd.

What we do know from the story is that, at some point in the episode, Zacchaeus admitted that he was a sinner and wanted to make things right. Jesus said that salvation happened that day. We do see that Zacchaeus showed incredible generosity.

SA – Zacchaeus was a wealthy man, a chief tax collector whose greedy ways changed. He became honest and generous. This head tax collector even humbled himself by saying he would admit to those he had wronged that he had lied to them and that he would restore to them four times the amount of money he had stolen. When we come to faith in Jesus and admit our sinfulness, we should show humility and a willingness to go back and generously correct past wrongs.

SAQ –
- Have you ever seen people whose lives have radically changed when they placed their faith in Jesus?
- If so, in what specific ways did their behavior change when they placed their faith in Jesus?
- What emotion and attitude would have to be inside of us to prompt us to go back to those we have wronged and to make amends?
- Have you ever seen someone who became a follower of Jesus who did go back and make up for past sins against people?
- What happened?

15. **SO** – At first it could be thought that Zacchaeus might have been trying to purchase spiritual acceptance from Jesus. But we know Zacchaeus came to faith in Jesus that day because Jesus said to him, "This day is salvation come to this house." Zacchaeus is the only person in the story who admitted he was a sinner and the only one in the story who gained salvation.

SA – Salvation cannot come to those who do not first admit to being sinners.

SAQ –
- We talked about whether or not Zacchaeus was trying to buy favor with Jesus. Today do people ever try to do good deeds or give money to impress God or to purchase God's favor?
- In what ways might they do that?
- Have you ever thought that way or known people who did?
- We saw that Zacchaeus was the only one in the story who admitted to being a sinner. And that he showed a genuine heart conversion by his change of heart toward money and toward other people. Also, Jesus verified that Zacchaeus' change was genuine toward God.
- Today do people struggle with admitting they are sinners?
- Based on this story, how important do you see confession of sin to be for people today?

16. **SO** – In the story, Jesus said directly to Zacchaeus, "This day is salvation come to this house." Jesus continued speaking and said, "seeing that Zacchaeus also is a son of Abraham." From this we see that others besides Zacchaeus were present. Also, by what Jesus said, we see that He changed who He was speaking to and Jesus was defending Zacchaeus to these people!

   SA – We saw Jesus working with Zacchaeus and Zacchaeus turning in faith to Jesus. But all the while, that critical crowd was there watching. Jesus was still reaching out to this self-righteous crowd, trying to get them to see themselves as needy and to open their minds to see that Zacchaeus was worthy of God's attention. Today there is still a self-righteous crowd that criticizes people whose lives change when they follow Jesus.

   SAQ –
   - Here was a person who no one liked who came to faith. And then Jesus defended this unpopular person to the self-righteous crowd. Today, does it ever happen that people are looked down on by others because of lifestyle or profession?
   - What kinds of people would be looked on as sinners by others, especially looked down on by those who are self-righteous?
   - Have you ever seen this kind of thing happen?
   - If you did see it, were the self-righteous people wanting to see the "sinner" seek spiritual assistance—to meet with Jesus, so to speak?
   - Jesus didn't give up on the crowd. What does this mean to you?

17. **SO** – Jesus' statement, that the purpose of His coming "is to seek and to save that which is lost," definitely honored Zacchaeus and seems to be a summary statement that criticized the crowd.

   SA – If we want approval by God, we need to admit our lostness and sinfulness and allow God to save us.

   SAQ –
   - What in Jesus' final short speech at the end of the story shows us today what God wants from us?
   - How many people in the world are capable of reaching that goal?
   - Is admitting our lostness and sinfulness a hard or easy thing to do?
   - Did we pick up anything from the story that shows us why some people who hear Jesus do not come to faith in Him?
   - What does this story speak to you?

18. **SO** – At first, it is obvious that Zacchaeus was seeking Jesus. Then part way through the story, it becomes a story of Jesus seeking out Zacchaeus!

SA – We saw in the story that Zacchaeus did seek Jesus, but also Jesus did seek Zacchaeus. Both are true. We must seek God. But know, at the same time, He seeks us.

SAQ –
- Is it true that people need to seek God?
- Do you see anything in the story about God seeking people?
- So which is it? Does God seek people or do people seek God?
- Is this a contradiction?
- How do you explain this?

Appendix C: User Impact Reports: Mentoring and Multiplication

"I am non-literate but serving the Lord as Pastor and Evangelist since 5 years. I came to the Lord in the year 1993 and I wanted to serve the Lord and to get Bible knowledge in any Bible College, but Academic Bible colleges did not accepted me to get Bible training because I am non-literate and also I was not able to understand God's messages on the pulpit because it was literate style.

"I was struggling to share the Gospel to my family members and friends; in this situation our Lord brought TGSP into our lives and ministry I thank God for that. I have learned 155 stories through STS method and now I am happy to say that I can share the Gospel to both the literate and non-literate."

Y. Babu - Evangelist/Pastor MMBC-Karnataka, India

"Imagine a group of people from any culture, most any age, believers and unbelievers, actively engaged, seeking out and discovering the treasures found in God's Word. Now you have a snapshot of what usually happens in a *Simply The Story* study group.

"We have applied STS on the mission field, in adult home Bible Studies, and in our children's and youth ministries. STS concepts impacted my sermons."

Pastor Chris Johnson - Calvary Chapel, USA

"*Simply The Story* is a God given technique to the church globally for the fulfillment of the great commission in our time and age. Though we have remained with one way of opening the Word of God (expository preaching), for many centuries, we have seen certain of its limitations.

"Now after learning STS through this manual, I dare say that here is another better way of making disciples. STS has changed my worldview and opened my eyes to Scripture in a greater way. Though I see the significance of STS in my country of south Sudan where illiteracy is very high, I see its impact even to learned people like myself.

"I highly recommend this resource to all Christian leaders worldwide. I pray that TGSP will double its effort to take this training far and wide. This manual is your best starting point as you seek to pursue training through the certified instructors."

Rev. Daniel Chagai Gak - Anglican Church of Sudan

"I am a scholar and theologian of missions with an earned PhD. from Fuller Theological Seminary and have worked among highly literate people for years. But I had become fully aware of how much the modern Western education system had restricted me to 'left-brain' (analytical, propositional, lecture) forms of teaching.

"Through the dynamism of the *Simply the Story* approach, founded by Dorothy and the growing movement she leads, I was awakened again to the reality that The Master Teacher Jesus always taught using stories, even with the highly learned Torah scholars of His time. Becoming a practitioner of storytelling, *al a* STS, has transformed my ministry to the Jewish people.

"I needed to truly make the shift, to re-learn and to emerge from well-worn mental ruts, and to bring Scripture to life and impart it with impact.

"STS is helping to catalyze a retrieval of storytelling in the postmodern West as well as aiding the growth of the church among oral learners in the non-Western world. Every professional teacher would find profound enhancement of his or her calling through the power of story and Bible storytelling. I highly recommend STS as an avenue to reach that goal."

Bill Bjoraker, PhD - Professor of Judeo-Christian Studies
William Carey International University, USA

"While much of Christendom is chasing after a variety of social justice opportunities, a world remains that hungers and thirsts for true righteousness. That hunger and thirst can only be satisfied with the Word of God—Jesus Christ.

"The deep discipleship approach of *Simply the Story* brings the wonder and amazement of Jesus through with brilliance.

"We use STS for our grandchildren, for a devotional guide. Our church's pastors all trained in STS and now use in the small groups teaching youth. Our mission's pastor and committee are now committed and redirecting funding toward the development of STS programs and Oral Bible Schools in Africa.

"The opportunities to take these methods of inductive Bible Study, evangelism and discipleship continue to grow. We are currently being called into the American inner-city where hopelessness abounds because of the false saviors and gospels that the welfare state and other man-centered cults perpetuate. The true Gospel is the only hope. Because we can use the wisdom of our Lord's teaching approach, with STS we now have a 'package' that we believe the Lord will use to bring redemption and restoration to a broken culture."

Mark Sands – President Church Builder Foundation, Global

Mentoring and Multiplication

These first three testimonies came from men mentored deeply by the TGSP executive staff. Those they mentored have trained others – who are training others. Isn't this God's way?

A Bishop in Embu stood up and said this to me. "The church is in trouble, because we lack church fathers who are biblical... Please tell those who trained you, 'Thank you for empowering Bramuel to be a father to Bishops.'"

Bramuel Musya - CEO Straight Path Resources, Kenya

STS method helped us to train more spiritual leaders than before and multiplication is talking place in producing spiritual leaders and keeping them in the church and sending them to the mission field. His Word is for both literate and non-literate, both young and old. It is a complete spiritual meal to fellowship with our Triune God.

Dr. Mark Muniyappa - All India Council / TGSP-India

What words do I use to express my gratitude to you all? I am so much thankful to the Lord and to this tool *Simply The Story.* In my 20 year's ministry time, it is most useful that I ever came across. STS certainly helped me getting deeper and wider into the Word of God but it also has many applications in my organisational life. The lesson learnt from this is to look for choices before I made any decision and it also made my team farsighted to see the impact of our work.

Ramesh Sapkota – CEO Kingdom Investments Nepal,
Organisation Fighting against Human Trafficking

First of all I want to give all glory and heartily thanks for our all mighty Lord Christ Jesus and my co-prayer Elder brother Ramesh.

When I met him I was new in Christ and my ministry was just like new born baby. I needed Spiritual mother to continue nourishing me. Ramesh gave me STS training. This was the beginning. In that time we were very few people in Christ and had one fellowship that was very weak. He continued STS in my Church.

Now in very short time through the STS training God used to plant eight Church and this year we have planned to plant two new Churches.

I used STS method to multiply Church because of this reason wonderfully I got invitation to participate in the STS training not only me but to get the Chance my daughter Church leader he is using STS method better then me.

Thank you brother Ramesh, I was only a body of butterfly and now you are preparing me to complete butterfly!

Thanks to the Servant of the Lord those who have labored for the STS to Glorify His Name and to bless me and my ministry.

Ps. Krishna P. Ghimire - Asst. Gen. Secretary, National Churches Fellowship of Nepal

---

Appendix D: One Leader's Discovery
Missionary Among Unreached People in Closed Country

When I first heard of oral Bible teaching, I was not at all interested. I reasoned that we can't build a strong church - rooted in the Scriptures - from telling children's Bible stories. But when I was in the States at a missions conference, I stayed with a couple that teaches oral Bible skills all over the world. I peppered them with all kinds of questions, and even traveled with them so I could video a training session they were giving that weekend.

I have a strong commitment that the church, as well as individual believers, be grounded in the Word of God. One cannot merely be familiar with Scripture truths; he/she has to inductively exegete God's Word, and correctly divide the Word of Truth. Anything less than this is opening believers to syncretism and a whole host of problems.

My absolute commitment to inductive study and responsible exegesis has only increased over the years. It has not waned with the idea of oral Bible teaching, it has only increased.

I was struck with the possibilities of doing inductive, exegetical study in an oral fashion. Could it be possible? And, why would it be necessary?

First, why is it necessary? All the people who teach oral Bible skills provide their CDs and their video clips of testimonies that do a far better job than can I of explaining the necessity of oral Bible teaching.

A major turning point came, I think, with a report at the 2004 Lausanne Committee for World Evangelism meetings, that documented the overwhelming percentage of people in the world that are oral learners-even in highly "literate" societies, like the U.K. or the U.S. This is even more acute in places where people are not highly literate.

For 17 years our team has been working in the field. We have taken a very oral approach to evangelism—we use no literature at all—our teammates learn, memorize and give an oral gospel presentation. As a result, we have seen phenomenal results; many, many people have put their faith in Christ.

When we did follow up, however, we immediately switched to a very literate approach. We provided believers with a Bible, and met with them to read, study and learn how to inductively study the Scriptures. With this follow up approach, we were hitting our heads against a wall. New believers languished. They were not growing in their faith, had grown cold, and backslidden.

In one village we entered, about 20 people made genuine commitments to Christ. We emphasized reading the Scriptures, showing them how to inductively read it for themselves, as well as spending personal time with them, sharing our lives.

Today, none of them are what you'd call "following hard after Christ." Many of them wanted to, but after all this time it's like they never really took in God's Word. It didn't sink in. I don't think the reading and studies ever got through to them at all.

What's more—they **never took the Scriptures and shared it with others**. How in the world will we ever reach the unreached if those we minister to do not minister to others?

Teaching the Bible orally has, I believe, fundamental advantages. First, many people absorb Bible truths in a way that they wouldn't when we try to get them to read it. Secondly, people are much more likely to share these truths with others—this is the ultimate "reproducible ministry."

Another advantage for closed areas of the world is that people are not as likely to get in trouble with the authorities. I could go on, but again, all the CDs and video clips have been put together to show the strategic nature of this approach.

The second question is the most important to me, "Is it possible to teach the Word inductively and exegetically in an oral fashion?"

Many organizations have some kind of division that promotes and teaches oral Bible learning. Most of them are members of the International Orality Network (ION). And there are a few organizations that specifically specialize in oral Bible teaching. I looked at several, got their materials, watched their videos, etc.

I went to the home office of one and I asked them, "Who out of all the organizations is the best in teaching how to teach the Bible orally? And they said the organization "STS" or *Simply the Story*. I looked on their website, got their materials, and could see that there really was a difference.

The thing I liked most about them was that they actually teach inductively in oral form. They are as close to exegetical, oral, Bible study as you can get. I knew I found what I was looking for. Through Skype, I started talking with them.

Early in November we had two instructors come from *Simply the Story*, and they led a training sessions for five days. The first two days were for trainers (people we selected from our team) and then the next three days those who had just been trained, trained the rest of our team with the help of the STS instructors. This has given us tremendous momentum in the mission as we've now started to incorporate this method in our mission work.

We started using this immediately, and I am really pleased with the reports of how it has been going. This does not mean that we've stopped teaching inductive, exegetical studies of the written Word. Ha! Far from it; this is still crucial.

But what we are doing orally 1) fits well with our studies in the written Word, it does not replace them, 2) reaches many people who can't, or don't read, 3) is something that the rank and file people can do well, (*we are mobilizing the laity*), 4) is able to be shared far easier with others beyond those whom we minister directly to, i.e. it spreads, 5) is perhaps the safest way the Word can be prolific in a closed country, 6) ***is not dependant on any outside funds, devices or other resources!*** It is the most reproducible mission's strategy around.

Again, as I said, I looked into a lot of different organizations' variants of this, but many of them weren't really telling the Bible in oral form. *Simply the Story* really emphasizes telling the Bible *accurately*—taking a single passage of Scripture and verbalizing it in way that is not an off-the-wall paraphrase—so that what you are sharing really is the Word, *the oral Word*, in the same way we read *the written Word*.

The written Word of God is the Canon, it is the source. We must teach it and how to accurately interpret it. But, from the written Word we get the oral Word. When we teach the Bible orally, we have the Bible open to show that it is from the Bible, the written Word. So, we show people that Scripture is the source.

In the early church, men read *from the Scriptures* and people *listened*. When Paul sent his letters, he asked that it be *read aloud*. I was struck with a question in one of the CDs I picked up: "What percentage of people in the first century could read or write—at a time when "3000 were added unto their number" in a single day? The answer, I was told, was about 5%.

Biblical accuracy is one reason I liked *Simply the Story*. But the other is that they also teach people how to learn inductively. After the story is given, they ask people inductive questions about what they just heard. They get the people to verbalize observations, they ask questions to help them form accurate interpretations, and they get them to see for themselves how it applies in their own lives.

This really is a tremendous tool, well developed, and skillfully taught.

God's Story: From Creation to Eternity

We developed *Simply The Story* as a result of the powerful worldwide impact of STS's "parent," *God's Story*. This 80-minute panorama of the Bible covers major stories from the Old and New Testaments and is available in both audio and video formats. By 2011, *God's Story* had been produced in over 300 world languages.

A favorite use of *God's Story* is on solar-powered audio-players.

> A young boy in Sudan was furious with a classmate. So he brought a knife to school intending to kill the other boy. The class's teacher had just obtained a solar player with *God's Story* in their local mother tongue. That fateful day, the teacher played the story of Cain and Abel for the class.
>
> When the angry boy heard that Bible story, something happened. He took out his knife—and gave it to the teacher, confessing his plan! God had touched his heart. That day, the boy asked God to forgive all of his sins and accepted Jesus as his Savior.

God's Word speaks. We encourage all who use *Simply The Story*, to also make use of *God's Story* in the languages spoken by the people in their region.

People use *God's Story* on solar players, CDs and MP3s. The video version, with hundreds of original art reenactments, brings Bible stories alive. Many millions who have seen *God's Story* in person and on TV, have responded in faith to become followers of Jesus. Thousands of ministries and denominations use *God's Story*.

The one-storyteller design of *God's Story* enables listeners to retell the Bible content to others. Most importantly, those in oral cultures respond in faith when they hear "the whole story." Starting with Creation, the Fall of Man and God's Promise of a Savior to come, a foundation for true understanding of the Gospel is laid. We see the impact and power of *God's Story* both in evangelism and in discipleship.

Using *God's Story* on solar players with the *God's Story* flip chart (which has 150 panels of pictures from the video) turns village evangelists into mobile movie theaters! Added tools such as discussion guides, the script in book format and radio scripts provide users a wide range of ways to put *God's Story* in action.

www.Gods-Story.org | Info@Gods-Story.org

World Contacts

Africa: EAfrica@Gods-Story.org

Ethiopia: Ethiopia@SimplyTheStory.org

West Africa "French & English":
STSWestAfrica@SimplyTheStory.org

West Africa "French":
GSWAfrica@Gods-Story.org

Europe: BT@SimplyTheStory.org

India: IndiaDirector@Gods-Story.org

Nepal: Nepal@SimplyTheStory.org

South East Asia: Thailand@SimplyTheStory.org

"Spanish": LatinAmerica@SimplyTheStory.org

Oceania: Oceania@SimplyTheStory.org

Philippines: eb@SimplyTheStory.org

USA: info@SimplyTheStory.org